M000073456

Clarence Jordan's

COTTON PATCH
Gospel

Clarence Jordan's

COTTON PATCH
Gospel

Matthew and John

SMYTH&HELWYS
PUBLISHING, INCORPORATED   MACON, GEORGIA

Smyth & Helwys Publishing, Inc.
6316 Peake Road
Macon, Georgia 31210-3960
1-800-747-3016
©2004 by Smyth & Helwys Publishing
All rights reserved.
Printed in the United States of America.

The paper used in this publication meets the minimum requirements of
American National Standard for Information Sciences—
Permanence of Paper for Printed Library Materials.
ANSI Z39.48–1984. (alk. paper)
Jordan, Clarence.

The cotton patch gospel / by Clarence Jordan.

p. cm.

Originally published separately in 4 vols.:
The cotton patch version of Matthew and John, 1970;
The cotton patch version of Luke and Acts, 1969;
The cotton patch version of Paul's Epistles, 1968;
The cotton patch version of Hebrews and the general Epistles, 1973.

ISBN 1-57312-422-2 (v. 1)

1. Bible. N.T. Matthew–Paraphrases, English. 2. Bible. N.T. John–Paraphrases, English.
3. Bible. N.T. Luke–Paraphrases, English. 4. Bible. N.T. Acts–Paraphrases, English.
5. Bible. N.T. Epistles of Paul–Paraphrases, English.
6. Bible. N.T. Hebrews–Paraphrases, English.
7. Bible. N.T. Epistles–Paraphrases, English.
I. Title.

BS2577.J65 2004

225.5'209–dc22

2003026305

Table of Contents

Foreword

By Tom Key

In 1979 I was thinking something most actors think: "What to do next?" This was an especially keen interest because our second child was on the way and we had no insurance. I was completing a two-year national tour portraying C. S. Lewis in *C. S. Lewis On Stage*, a solo performance I had adapted from his writing. Because a theater in London had acquired worldwide rights to another one-man script on Lewis, I was not able to perform mine again for four years. My wife, one-and-a-half children, and I were living in Atlanta, Georgia. These were the practical circumstances of my search then. That was the necessity, which was, as it always is, going to be the "mother of invention."

More important, although I only perceive this in hindsight, was a spiritual necessity, a circumstance of my soul that was set on dramatizing the Christ story to see what God might have looked like and sounded like as a human being. Having grown up in the American South attending a Southern Baptist church, I couldn't reconcile the shock value of the original story with the mainstream acceptance it had acquired 2,000 years later in modern culture. How could millions of people over the world for two millennia attend meetings based on the belief that God had come, risen from the dead, and commanded us to love one

---

Tom Key conceived the one-man play *Cotton Patch Gospel of Matthew*, based on the paraphrases of Clarence Jordan, and in 1981 it developed into a musical co-authored with Russell Treyz and with a score and lyrics by Harry Chapin. It premiered at the Lamb's Theater, New York, and was awarded two Dramalogue Awards for Outstanding Achievement in Theater.

another, and then, instead of this global practice of accomplishing world peace, the human race appeared to be more than ever set on a course of destroying itself and the planet on which it existed?

It never occurred to me that the belief of Christendom was inaccurate, but when it came to relieving war, poverty, hunger, torture, murder, greed, rape, and prejudice, the details of the Incarnation appeared irrelevant, a curious myth that made for two good holidays in winter and spring. Perhaps the ritual form, which had been filled with the power of these miracles, had leaked. Perhaps it needs renewal every generation to successfully impact the present.

Interestingly, in the 1970s, the New Testament drove not only attendance for gatherings in churches at Christmas and Easter, but box-office business on and off Broadway for audiences to see *Godspell* and *Jesus Christ Superstar*. Here is where I had a personal collision with the zeitgeist, vocationally and professionally. The vision that these two musicals gave of the humanity of God was breathtaking. Surely these actors captured more of how Jesus' face must have looked than all the cinematic versions, which, to me, sent a strong visual message that holiness leaves a countenance similar to that of someone who has had a frontal lobotomy.

Still, the plot of these two plays borrowed heavily from the Gospels without paying honor to their dramatic conclusions. The Jesus of *Godspell* lives on in our memory much as George Washington or Dr. Martin Luther King Jr. The productions I have seen end with the actors carrying the crucified body of Jesus out on their shoulders, but joyously and triumphantly singing the last song of the musical, "Long Live God." And the story of Christ in *Jesus Christ Superstar* stops with the crucifixion. That sort of makes a big difference, similar to what a different movie Steven Spielberg could have made if *E.T.* never went home and the last frame of the picture was the once adorable creature laying there cold, stiff, and dead. Elliott would have certainly grown up to be a different person.

Before one of my last performances for the next four years of *C. S. Lewis On Stage* in Des Moines, Iowa, I was having dinner with the producer when I spotted a postcard advertisement he had received as notice that Alec McGowan would appear at the Guthrie Theater in *Saint Mark's Gospel*, a performance renowned by theater critics in London and New York. McGowan had memorized and performed the entire Gospel in the King James Version. What struck me, being from Birmingham, Alabama, was "I could do that from a down-home approach." My next thought was, "But it would probably be a one-joke idea lacking in authenticity because I couldn't actually translate the original Greek." When I casually expressed my idea to the producer, he introduced me to the work and life of Clarence Jordan.

He said there was actually a person in Georgia, in the mid-20th century, with degrees in agriculture and New Testament Greek, qualifying with a Masters of Divinity to be a Southern Baptist pastor, who instead had started a farming community where black people and white people worked, studied, worshiped, and lived together. Immediately, I understood that here was an individual who must have banked his life on the belief that Jesus was still alive.

Within two weeks, I was graciously received at Koinonia Farm where I was given a tour, stories, and more books, articles, and sermons than I could have imagined. I could have sworn the Christ of the Roman Empire was breathing down my neck in the Bible Belt. In two more months, after creating a one-man dramatization based on Clarence Jordan's paraphrases of the Gospels, I was performing *Cotton Patch Gospel* at colleges in Tennessee, Iowa, and California. In another year, I had portrayed, in more than fifty states, a Jesus who comes back from the dead real enough to have a cup of coffee and a slice of pecan pie with his followers.

Not only did Clarence's application of his New Testament Greek scholarship to the practical work of his life, with all of its consequent suffering and reward, provide a trustworthy map for plotting the place and time of this dramatization, but his insight into the character of Judas was critical for illuminating what would be the pivotal crisis of this story. It is a crisis that, instead of letting us—2,000 years later—off the moral hook, slams us right back into the pressure of the decision we still must make with much the same spiritual equipment: "Choose you this day whom you will serve."

September 1981: I'm walking down West 44th Street in New York City on my way to a press interview for the upcoming off-Broadway premiere of *Cotton Patch Gospel.* Harry Chapin wrote the music, his last after a career as one of the great American folk singers and one of the great humanitarians, having raised more than 5 million dollars for World Hunger. Walking briskly next to me is our publicist. She is a native New Yorker and a Jew. I come from Alabama and am a Christian.

PUBLICIST: So, I've wanted to tell you something I've been thinking about this play.
ME: Shoot.
PUBLICIST: I think *Godspell* and *Jesus Christ Superstar* are both about a man who became a God, but *Cotton Patch Gospel* is about a God who became a man.

April 2003: I've performed the play as I originally conceived it—a one-man dramatization—and as a musical, with a cast ranging from five to sixteen actor/musicians, in ten productions for more than 1,000 performances (when I reached my fortieth birthday, I stopped counting), from New York to Los Angeles and Atlanta to Vancouver. The musical has been published by Dramatic Publishing Company and still receives numerous productions across North America. Recently, a twenty-three-year-old from North Carolina produced it in Charlotte and on opening night raised $15,000 for Habitat for Humanity in El Salvador. I've had people tell me they reentered ministry or service work, got off drugs, or broke through suicidal depression as a result of seeing this musical. I've also seen full-page ads warning the community to stay away from this "blasphemy"; heard from students in a Catholic college production pleading with me to persuade their bishop to reverse his decision to close down the play and instead perform *Godspell* because an anonymous caller reported to him that it was sacrilegious; and received a nervous call from the stage manager of a tour performing it the next afternoon in an outdoor theater in Montgomery because the Klan planned to be positioned in the surrounding woods to shoot the actor for linking the KKK to the lynching of Jesus—the next day, the performance was cancelled, not because the actors backed down, but because a downpour rained out the theater.

Certainly, over two decades, a lot more happens than the course of one play. The globe turns, galaxies revolve, stars flame out, hearts beat. Friends die, including Harry Chapin, and new friends are given. Parents are lost, and children are born. Addiction, disease, accident, war and mental illness take many. Many recover, escape, get sane. Marriage multiplies two people by thirty years. and in a room of a hundred people she's still the one. Three baby boys become three brilliant young men in about two weeks. Two towers and an era violently end. Habitat for Humanity, founded by Millard Fuller, inspired by Clarence Jordan, creates affordable housing around the world.

But for this moment, you have come to read this book. Congratulations and get ready. Here is what I hope for you: It's about what the publicist said twenty-one years ago comparing three contemporary musicals based on the life of Jesus. We can try to reach toward God, and we can also try to receive how God is reaching us. This is an effort that I don't think is exclusive to a certain religion, political platform, nationality, or class. It is a human enterprise. That's why I believe it is best illuminated and practiced in the context that can connect people across the boundaries of race, religion, or creed, in the common truths of the human experience made clear and visible by the artistic event. That's why I regard all story, all literature, comic or tragic, as a matter of what is meant by the word "gospel"—that is, good news.

Once upon a time, a Cotton Patch bass player, raised a Pentecostal, for whom we had to have a spittoon on stage and who had played with the likes of Flatt and Scruggs at the Grand Ol' Opry, said to me, "You know, when I first heard how you were telling this story, I thought, 'Humph, That's sacrilegious.' But then I thought, 'It's the Truth.'" I was playing John the Baptizer that night, and I answered him, "Can I hear a 'Hallelujah?!'"

Introduction

By Millard Fuller

I had the wonderful and blessed privilege of knowing Clarence Jordan personally. I first met him when my wife Linda and I, along with our two children, Chris and Kim, went to Koinonia Farm in December 1966 at a time of deep personal crisis. Linda and I had decided to leave our life of affluence in Montgomery, Alabama—to divest ourselves of our wealth—and to seek a life of Christian service.

When we arrived at Koinonia, a Christian communal farm near Americus, Georgia, I had never heard of Clarence Jordan and I knew practically nothing about Koinonia.

Within a few hours of our arrival, I strongly sensed God's presence there and Linda and I both felt that God had directed us to that special place. Our intended visit of a couple of hours lasted a month. Clarence and others at Koinonia were so encouraging and supportive to Linda and me as we were seeking to know and follow God's will. They affirmed us and gave us spiritual strength for the great change in our lives at that time.

Clarence Jordan captivated me. I had never met anyone quite like him in my life. He was incredibly intelligent. When he

---

Millard Fuller is the founder and president of Habitat for Humanity International. Fuller's business expertise and entrepreneurial drive made him a millionaire by age 29. Then, after a rededication of his life to family and to following God's path, Fuller and his wife, Linda, decided to sell their possessions and give the money to the poor. Following missions work in Africa, the Fullers moved to Koinonia Farm, the birthplace of Habitat for Humanity. Fuller has written nine books, most recently two volumes titled *Building Materials for Life*.

spoke, everyone listened. The man had something to say. And what he said was so focused of things of the spirit. He related almost everything to God and to God's presence and activity in the world.

Clarence's favorite topic was "the God Movement." He reminded his listeners that Americans weren't familiar with "kingdoms" so it was problematical to understand "the kingdom of God." But, he said, people in this country are familiar with the concept of a movement, such as the women's liberation movement, the civil rights movement, and so forth. Clarence said God had a movement underway and that God wanted people to be a part of it.

He said the principal problem of modern Christians was that they wanted God to conform to their agenda—to bless their endeavors and goals. Clarence said that was backwards. God has an agenda and wants God's people to learn what it is and to become *active* participants in that agenda. Hence, the expression "the God movement."

Concerning church congregations, Clarence said they often built "God boxes." Then they would invite a certain kind of God into their "boxes." That God, for instance, might be a God for white people, affluent people, or highly educated people. But guess what? The God of all creation, the God of the universe, the Father of the Lord Jesus Christ, doesn't show up in human made boxes. That God, the authentic Lord of All, is shut out.

Clarence thundered against such things. As we listened to him, there was a quiet "yes, yes, yes!" ringing in the heart and mind even as a tinge of apprehension rose up in the throat. We realized that if we acted upon what Clarence was saying, there might well be negative consequences.

The overriding feeling in my soul as I talked with Clarence Jordan was that he was an authentic person, full of grace and kindness, imbued with a dynamic faith, committed to being faithful to Christ, *no matter what*. I was often nearly breathless as

Introduction

I listened to this great and humble man of God. I felt so privileged to be in his presence and to learn from him.

Clarence Jordan was a man of *relevance*. He made God's word relevant. Every situation in life was measured against the life and teachings of Christ. Clarence was aware of culture and tradition, but his life was lived out in obedience to the claims of Christ, even when those claims caused him to violate culture and tradition.

His *Cotton Patch* translations are one of the many contributions Clarence made to the world in helping people understand the message of the New Testament in the context of the world where people actually live.

For example, in the Bible, the story of the Good Samaritan involves a Jew, a Samaritan, and an unnamed victim of a robbery on a lonely road in the Middle East, and it took place 2,000 years ago. In the *Cotton Patch* translation, the Jew becomes a white man, the Samaritan becomes an African American, and the crime victim is robbed and beaten in Ellaville, Georgia.

Everyone loves the biblical account of that story. It is such a wonderful story, a safe distance away and a long time ago. Clarence puts the story "in your face." He puts it up close and relevant to our situation. That's the power of the Cotton Patch translations. The retelling of the well-known stories from Matthew, Luke, John, and other New Testament books are often amusing, but also jarring and disturbing.

Whether in person or through his writings, Clarence Jordan was not and is not a person to be ignored. To do so is to imperil our souls.

This humble man of the soil, whose usual dress was a denim shirt and blue jeans, was close to God, and he was steadfast and faithful to God throughout his life.

I not only had the great privilege of knowing Clarence Jordan personally. I also had the privilege of being with him minutes after his sudden death at age fifty-seven, on October 29, 1969. (Our family had moved to Koinonia in 1968.) He was writing a sermon to be delivered at Mercer University when God called him home. He was at work in his "writing shack" out in the field about a hundred yards from the main cluster of community buildings at Koinonia. He had a massive heart attack. He just leaned his head against the wall and was gone.

When I walked in and saw that he was obviously dead, I was filled with sadness but then with joy, realizing that he had gone home to be with the Lord he served so faithfully in his lifetime. I started exclaiming out loud, "You made it, Clarence. You made it!"

The next day, when we buried him, dressed in his blue jeans and lovingly placed in a simple pine box, our little two-year-old daughter Faith, who had been born out of the reconciliation between Linda and me, stepped to the edge of the grave as we lowered his body into the red Georgia clay and started singing the only song she knew: "Happy birthday, Clarence. Happy birthday to you!"

In the years since the death of Clarence Jordan, his influence has continued to grow. In a real sense, he was and is the spiritual father of Habitat for Humanity. His powerful presence and message of the relevant gospel inspire me still today. And his life and teachings continue to inspire thousands of other people all across the United States and in many other lands.

I encourage you to open your heart and mind as you read these pages. Hear the voice and spirit of Clarence Jordan as he makes the "old, old story" come to life for you. Get ready to be changed. As Clarence often said, "God's new order of the spirit is confronting you and challenging you."

As you read, you *will be* challenged and confronted. What will be your response? I hope it is in the direction of obedience and faithfulness in the context of where you are in your life *right now!*

A Note on
The Cotton Patch Gospel—Matthew and John

By Clarence Jordan

PUBLISHER'S NOTE: *At the time of his death, in October, 1969, Clarence Jordan had completed translating, and had polished for publication the Gospel of Matthew and the first eight chapters of the Gospel of John. That manuscript was on his desk when he died. But the Introduction for it had not yet been written. In the Introductions to his two previous volumes, however, he had explained his purposes in making these "cotton patch" translations, described some of the difficulties he had faced in doing this work, and had stated his hopes of what the reader would find in these colloquial versions of the familiar New Testament passages. The following paragraphs, taken from these two previous Introductions, will provide the new reader with the background needed for appreciating Clarence Jordan and his work.*

The purpose of the "cotton patch" approach to the scriptures is to help the modern reader have the same sense of participation in them which the early Christians must have had. This approach is explained in detail in the first volume of this series [*The Cotton Patch Gospel—Paul's Epistles*]. By stripping away the fancy language, the artificial piety, and the barriers of time and distance, this version puts Jesus and his people in the midst of our modern world, living where we live, talking as we talk, working, hurting, praying, bleeding, dying, conquering, alongside the rest of us. It seeks to restore the original feeling and excitement of the fast-breaking *news*—good news—rather than musty history.

To be sure, this is a risky undertaking. For one thing, it simply can't be done with absolute accuracy. Matching present-day people, groups and settings with their biblical counterparts involves a good bit of guesswork and subjective interpretation, mingled with the best knowledge one has of both the modern and ancient situation. For example, I have paired the Pharisees with church members, and the scribes with theologians and seminary professors. This may pinch, and may well be challenged. In fact, I gladly yield to those who may do a better job of matching.

Likewise, there just isn't any word in our vocabulary which adequately translates the Greek word for "crucifixion." *Our* crosses are so shined, so polished, so respectable that to be impaled on one of them would seem to be a blessed experience. We have thus emptied the term "crucifixion" of its original content of terrific emotion, of violence, of indignity and stigma, of defeat. I have translated it as "lynching," well aware that this is not technically correct. Jesus was officially tried and legally condemned, elements generally lacking in a lynching. But having observed the operation of Southern "justice," and at times having been its victim, I can testify that more people have been lynched "by judicial action" than by unofficial ropes. Pilate at least had the courage and the honesty publicly to wash his hands and disavow all legal responsibility. "See to it yourselves," he told the mob. And they did. They crucified him in Judea and they strung him up in Georgia, with a noose tied to a pine tree.

But admitting the risks, perhaps the rewards will more than offset them. Possibly the wind of Pentecost will blow through our houses, and its fire enkindle our hearts. Maybe Jesus, the great interpreter of the scriptures, will join us and enlighten us on our journey from Atlanta to Austell even as he did the two disciples on their way from Jerusalem to Emmaus. He may let us sit at his feet and wash them with our tears. Perhaps he'll startle us with his parables and powerful sermons, and sting us with his honest rebukes. He may come alive. And we too.

Matthew

1.

[The first seventeen verses of Matthew consist of Jesus' family tree. Since this purely historical material has already been well translated, and because nothing would be gained by merely modernizing the names, we are omitting it.]

18. The beginning of Jesus the Leader was like this: While his mama, Mary, was engaged to Joseph, but before they had relations, she was made pregnant by the Holy Spirit. Since Joseph, her fiancé, was a considerate man and didn't want to make a public scandal, he decided to quietly break up with her. As he was wondering about the whole situation, a messenger from the Lord came to him in a dream and said, "Joe Davidson, don't be ashamed to marry Mary, because the Holy Spirit has made her pregnant. Now she'll give birth to a boy, who you'll name Jesus,[1] because he will deliver his nation from their errors."

22. This whole event was the completion of what the Lord had said through the prophet: "Listen, a young lady will get pregnant and give birth to a boy, and they'll name him 'God-is-with-us.'"

24. Then Joseph woke up and did as the Lord's messenger had directed—he married his girl. But he didn't sleep with her until she had her baby. And he did name it Jesus.

2.

1. When Jesus was born in Gainesville, Georgia, during the time that Herod was governor, some scholars from the Orient came to Atlanta and inquired, "Where is the one who was born to be governor of Georgia? We saw his star in the Orient, and we came to honor him." This news put Governor Herod and all his Atlanta cronies in a tizzy. So he called a meeting of the big-time preachers and politicians, and asked if they had any idea where the Leader was to be born. "In Gainesville, Georgia," they replied, "because there's a Bible prophecy which says:

'And you, Gainesville, in the state of Georgia,
Are by no means the least in the Georgia delegation;
From you will come forth a governor,
Who will wisely guide my chosen people.'"

7. Then Herod called in the scholars privately and questioned them in detail about the exact time of the star's appearance. And he sent them off to Gainesville with this instruction: "Go and find out the facts about the child. Then tell me what you've learned, so that I too may come and honor him." They listened to the governor and left. And you know, the star which they saw in the Orient went ahead of them until it came and stood above the place where the child was. (Just looking at the star flooded them with great happiness.) So they went inside the house and saw the baby with his mother, Mary. They bowed down and honored him, and opened the presents they had brought to him—gifts of jewelry, incense, and perfume. And having gotten the word in a dream not to revisit Herod, they went back to their own country by another route.

13. After they had checked out, the Lord's messenger made connection with Joseph in a dream and said, "Get moving, and take your wife and baby and highball it to Mexico. Then stay put until I get word to you, because Herod is going to do his best to kill the baby." So he got right up, took the baby and its mother and checked out by night for Mexico. He stayed there until the death of Herod. (This gave meaning to what the Lord said through the prophet: "I summoned my son from Mexico.")

16. Then it dawned on Herod that he had been duped by the learned men, and he really blew his top. He gave orders to kill all the babies in Gainesville and thereabouts who were under two, on the basis of the schedule which he had obtained from the scholars. (Then the saying of Jeremiah the prophet was given meaning:

> "A noise is heard in Ramah,
> Great weeping and anguish;
> Rachel is grieving for her children
> And there's no consoling her,
> Because she has lost them.")

19. Now when Herod passed away, the Lord's messenger contacted Joseph in Mexico by a dream. "Get moving," he said, "and take the child and his mother and return to the South, for the people who were trying to take the boy's life have died."

21. So he packed up and took the child and his mother, and returned to the South. He heard that Herod's boy Archelaus was governor of Alabama and so he was scared to settle down there. He was given instruction in a dream to go on over into south Georgia to the city of Valdosta. (This gave meaning to the prophet's word: "He shall be called a Valdostan.")

3.

1. One day John the Baptizer showed up and started preaching in the rural areas of Georgia. "Reshape your lives," he said, "because God's new order of the Spirit is confronting you. This is what the prophet Isaiah meant when he said,

> 'A voice is shouting in the rurals:
> Lay out the Lord's highway;
> Straighten his roads.'"

4. This guy John was dressed in blue jeans and a leather jacket, and he was living on corn bread and collard greens. Folks were coming to him from Atlanta and all over north Georgia and the backwater of the Chattahoochee. And as they owned up to their crooked ways, he dipped them in the Chattahoochee.

7. When John noticed a lot of Protestants and Catholics showing up for his dipping, he said to them, "You sons of snakes, who put the heat on you to run from the fury about to break over your heads? You must give some *proof* that you've had a change of heart. And don't think that you can feed yourselves that 'we-good-white-people' stuff, because I'm telling you that if God wants to he can make white folks out of this pile of rocks. Already the chain saw is set at the trunk of the trees, and every tree that doesn't perform some worthwhile function is sawed down and burned up. I am indeed dipping you in water into a changed life; the one who follows me is so much stronger than I that I'm unworthy to shine his shoes. *He* will dip you in Holy Spirit and fire. His combine is already running and he'll give the field a thorough going-over. He'll store the grain in his bin and burn off the stubble."

13. Then Jesus arrived at the Chattahoochee from south Georgia, to be dipped by John. But John tried to put him off. "Look," he said, "*I* ought to be dipped by *you*, yet *you* are coming to *me*." Jesus replied, "Please let me be baptized right now, for it is proper for us to give meaning in this way to all that's right." Then John consented. Now when Jesus was immersed and just as he came up from the water, the sky was split and he saw God's Spirit settling upon him like a dove alighting. And you know, a voice spoke from the sky, "This is my dear Son; I'm proud of him."

4.

1. Then Jesus was taken by the Spirit into the country, to be given a test by the Confuser. And after a forty-day fast he was plenty hungry. Well, the Confuser came around and said to him, "So you're God's Head Man, huh? Then order these stones to become pones." But Jesus told him, "The Scripture says,

> 'A man shall not live on a pone alone,
> But on every word falling from the lips of God.'"

5. Next, the Confuser takes him into Atlanta and stands him on the steeple of First Church and says to him, "Okay, let's suppose you're God's Head Man; now, jump down from here, for the Scripture says,

> 'He will make his angels responsible for you, And they'll carry you along on their hands, To keep you from stumping your toe on a stone.'"

Jesus replied, "Yes, but it is also written, 'You shall not try God's patience!'"

8. Again, the Confuser gets him way up on a high mountain and points out to him all the nations in the world and their splendor, and he says to Jesus, "Now if you'll just let *me* be boss, I'll turn all this over to you." Then Jesus tells him, "Scram, Satan! The Scripture says,' You shall let the Lord God be your boss, and you shall give your loyalty to him alone.'" At that the Confuser leaves him, and you know, angels came and began waiting on him.

12. Now when Jesus learned that John had been arrested, he set out for south Georgia. Then he moved from Valdosta and located in Savannah, which is on the coast in Chatham County

and next to Effingham. (This gave meaning to the words spoken
by the prophet Isaiah:

> "County of Chatham and County of Effingham
> Across the Chattahoochee, beside the sea,
> State of Georgia, land of blacks;
> The people who operated under cover of night
> Had their eyes opened and saw a great light;
> The sun arose on the dwellers in the land of darkness
> and death.")

17. From then on, Jesus began spreading his ideas. "Reshape
your lives, for God's new order of the Spirit is confronting you."

18. As he was walking beside Lake Lanier, he saw two brothers, Simon (who was nicknamed Rock) and Andrew, putting out
a net in the lake, since they were fishermen. He says to them,
"Y'all come with me, and I'll train you to net people." And right
away they left their fishing gear and walked with him. A little
further on he saw two more brothers, Jim and Jack Zebedee, in
the boat with their father, getting their nets in shape. He invited
them, and right away they left the boat and their father, and
walked with him.

23. And he traveled throughout Georgia, teaching in their
churches and spreading the good news of the new order, and
healing every sickness and disease that people had. News of him
spread through the whole South. Folks brought to him all who
were ill with various diseases and afflictions—the demonized, the
lunatics, and the paralyzed—and he made them well. Large
crowds from all over Georgia, Florida, Alabama, and Tennessee
followed him.

5.

1. When Jesus saw the large crowd, he went up the hill and sat down. His students gathered around him, and he began teaching them. This is what he said:

"The spiritually humble are God's people, for they are citizens of his new order.

"They who are deeply concerned are God's people, for they will see their ideas become reality.

"They who are gentle are his people, for they will be his partners across the land.

"They who have an unsatisfied appetite for the right are God's people, for they will be given plenty to chew on.

"The generous are God's people, for they will be treated generously.

"Those whose motives are pure are God's people, for they will have spiritual insight.

"Men of peace and good will are God's people, for they will be known throughout the land as his children.

"Those who have endured much for what's right are God's people; they are citizens of his new order.

"You all are God's people when others call you names, and harass you and tell all kinds of false tales on you just because you follow me. Be cheerful and good-humored, because your spiritual advantage is great. For that's the way they treated men of conscience in the past.

13. "You all are the earth's salt. But now if you just sit there and don't salt, how will the world ever get salted? You'll be so worthless that you'll be thrown out and trampled on by the rest of society. You all are the world's light; you are a city on a hill that cannot be hid. Have you ever heard of anybody turning on a light and then covering it up? Don't you fix it so that it will light up the whole room? Well then, since you are God's light which he has turned on, go ahead and shine so clearly that when your conduct is observed it will plainly be the work of your spiritual Father.

17. "Don't ever think that I'm trying to destroy the moral and religious principles of our way of life. My purpose is not to destroy them but to establish them. For I truthfully tell you that as long as heaven and earth remain, not one dotting of an 'i' or crossing of a 't' will be eliminated from our highest and noblest ideals until every one of them becomes a reality. So then, if anyone disregards one of the least of these God-given principles, and encourages others to do so, he shall be considered unimportant in God's new order of the Spirit. But whoever lives by them and upholds them shall be considered vital to God's new order of the Spirit.

20. "And let me tell you something else: Unless your conduct is better than that of usual, ordinary religious people, you will never make the grade into God's new order of the Spirit. For example, you have always been told, 'Don't murder,' and 'If anybody does murder, he shall be brought to judgment.' But I'm telling you that everyone who nurses a grudge against his fellow man shall be brought into judgment. And anyone who spits in the face of his brother man stands condemned, and whoever yells, 'You low-down so-and-so!' shall be roasted in hell's fires. So then, if you are in worship services and keep remembering all the things your brother has against you, leave the sanctuary and go look up the one you have wronged and straighten things out with him. Only then may you return to church.

25. "Be courteous at all times towards an opponent. Otherwise, you might be dragged into court, turned over to the sheriff and thrown into the clink. I'm telling you a fact, you won't get out of there until you have paid the last cent of your fine.

27. "You've heard it said, 'Don't sleep with someone you're not married to.' But I want to tell you, whoever sets his eye on a woman with the hope of intercourse with her has already slept with her in his mind. So if your right eye becomes hopelessly infected, have it cut out and thrown away, because it is better to lose one of your organs than to lose your body. Or if your right hand becomes hopelessly infected, cut it off and throw it away, because it is better to lose one of your limbs than to lose your body.[2]

31. "It has also been said, 'If a man divorces his wife, let him give her a certificate that she is free.' But I'm telling you all, anybody who divorces his wife, except for sleeping with another man, causes her to have had unlawful intercourse, and whoever marries one so divorced also has unlawful intercourse.

33. "Again you have heard it said by the old folks, 'Don't break your oath, and always keep a solemn oath to the Lord.' But I'm telling you not to make any oaths at all—not by the heaven, as God's throne; or by the earth, as his foot-rest; or by Atlanta, as 'the city of the governor.' Don't make an oath even by your head, because you can't make one hair white or black. Instead, let your word be a straightforward 'yes' or 'no.' If it takes more than that, it's bad.

38. "You've also heard the saying, 'Take an eye for an eye; take a tooth for a tooth.' But I'm telling you, *never* respond with evil. Instead, if somebody slaps you on your right cheek, offer him the other one too. And if anybody wants to drag you into court and take away your shirt, let him have your undershirt. If somebody makes you go a mile for him, go two miles. Give to him who asks of you, and don't turn your back on anyone who wants a loan.

43. "Another thing you've always heard is, 'Love your own group and hate the hostile outsider,' But I'm telling you, love the outsiders and pray for those who try to do you in, so that you might be sons of your spiritual Father. For he lets his sun rise on both sinners and saints, and he sends rain on both good people and bad. Listen here, if you love only those who love you, what's your advantage? Don't even scalawags do that much? And if you speak to no one but your friends, how are you any different? Don't the non-Christians do as much? Now you, you all must be mature, as your spiritual Father is mature.

6.

1. "See to it that your effort to do right is not based on a desire to be popular. If it is, you'll get no help from your spiritual Father. For instance, when you make a gift to charity, don't make a lot of noise about it, like the phonies do at church and at civic clubs, so as to be praised by their cronies. The truth is, such praise is all they'll get out of it. But you, when you give to charity, don't pat yourself on the back, so that your gift might be truly secret. And your Father, who sees secrets, will respond to you.

5. "And when you pray, don't be like the phonies. For they love to stand up and pray in church and at public occasions, so they might build a reputation as pray-ers. The truth is, that's all they'll get out of it. But you, when you pray, go to your bedroom, shut the door, and pray to your Father in private. And your Father, who sees the inner life, will respond to you. And while you are praying, don't jabber like pagans, who think that their long-windedness will get them an answer. Don't you be like them, for your Father knows what you need before you ever ask him. So here's the way you all should pray:

'Father of us, O Spiritual One,
Your Name be truly honored.
Your Movement spread, your will prevail
Through earth, as through the heavens.
Grant us sustaining bread each day.
Forgive our debts as we forgive
The debts of all who cannot pay.
And from confusion keep us clear;
Deliver us from evil's sway.'

"For if you forgive men when they wrong you, your spiritual Father will forgive you, too. But if you don't forgive others, neither will your Father forgive your wrongs.

16. "Now when you go to church, don't be like the religious phonies who put on a solemn face to impress men with their piety. Rather, when you go to church, act perfectly normal so as not to give the impression you're going there to be seen, but to worship God. And your Father, who sees the inner life, will respond to you.

19. "Put no value on earthly things, which worms and rust consume, and which thieves break into and steal. Rather, y'all set your hearts on spiritual values, which neither worms nor rust consume, and which thieves do not break into and steal. For your values and your character are wrapped up together.

22. "The body depends on the eyes for light. Now if your eyes are in focus, then the body will have clear light. But if your eyes are not in focus,[3] then your whole body will be in confused darkness. Now if your life is so divided, you're *really* in the dark! That's why it is impossible for a man to serve *two* masters. For he will hate one of them and love the other; he will have respect for one and contempt for the other! It is *impossible* to be in bondage to both God and money.

25. "Therefore, let me tell you all something: Don't worry about making a living—what you'll eat, what you'll drink, what you'll wear. Isn't the life of a man more important than what he eats? Think for a moment about the birds of the sky. They don't plant. They don't harvest. They don't store up in barns. Even so, your spiritual Father cares for them. Really now, aren't you all more precious than *birds*? Besides, who of you, by fretting and fuming, can make himself one inch taller?

28. "And what's all this big to-do over clothing? Look yonder at that field of flowers, how they're growing. They do no housework and no sewing. But I'm telling you, not even Solomon in all his finery was ever dressed up like one of them. Well then, if God so clothes the flowers of the field, which are blooming today and are used for kindling tomorrow, won't he do even more for you, you spiritual runts? So cut out your anxious talk about 'what are we gonna eat, and what are we gonna drink, and what are we gonna wear.' For the people of the world go tearing around after all *these* things. Listen, your spiritual Father is quite aware that you've got to have all such stuff. Then set your heart on the God Movement and its kind of life, and all these things will come as a matter of course. Don't worry over the future; let the future worry over itself. Each day has enough trouble of its own.

7.

1. "Don't preach just to keep from being preached to. For the same sermon you preach will be applied to you, and the stuff you dish out to others will be dished up to you. Why examine the splinter in your brother's eye, and take no notice of the plank in your own eye? Or how can you say to your brother, 'Bud, hold still while I pick that splinter out of your eye,' when there is a plank in yours? Listen, you phony, first pull the plank from your eye and then you'll be able to see better to get the splinter out of your brother's eye.

> "'Don't throw your valuables to the dogs,
> And don't spread your pearls before the hogs;
> Or they will trample them under their feet
> And even turn and bite you.'

7. "Start asking and it will be given to you; start looking and you will find; start knocking, and the door will be opened to you. For every asker receives, and every seeker finds, and to everyone who knocks the door shall be opened. Is there any man among you whose son shall ask him for bread and he'll give him a rock? So if you, weak mortals that you are, are capable of making good gifts to your children, don't you think your spiritual Father will give even better gifts to those who ask him?

12. "Therefore, in all your dealings with people, treat them as you want to be treated. This, in a nutshell, is the essence of all our moral and religious principles.

13. "Approach life through the gate of discipline. For the way that leads to emptiness is wide and easy, and a lot of folks are taking that approach. But the gate into the full life is hard, and the road is bumpy, and only a few take this route.

15. "Keep your eye peeled for fake preachers, who come to you with sheepskins from wolf-schools. You'll be able to distinguish them by the way they live. You know, you don't gather pecans from a persimmon tree nor peaches from a chinaberry, do you? So it is, a cultivated tree makes cultivated fruit, and a wild tree makes wild fruit. It is impossible for a cultivated tree to bear wild fruit, or for a wild tree to bear cultivated fruit. Any tree that does not produce cultivated fruit is chopped down and thrown into the fire. That's why I told you that you could know them by the way they *live*.

21. "Not everyone who glibly calls me 'Lord, Lord,' shall enter the God Movement, but he who *does* the will of my spiritual Father. The time will come when many people will gather around and say, 'L-o-ord, oh L-o-o-rd, *we* sure did preach in your name, didn't we? And in your name *we* gave the devil a run for his money, didn't we? *We* did all kinds of stunts in your name, didn't we?' Then I'll admit right in front of everybody, 'I've never known you. Get away from me, you wicked religious racketeers.'

24. "That's why the man who hears these words of mine and acts on them shall be like a wise man who built his house on the rock. Down came the rain, up rose the floods, out lashed the winds. They all cut at that house, but it didn't fall. It was on *rock* foundation.

26. "And the man who hears these words of mine and fails to act on them shall be like an idiot who built his house on the sand. The rain came down, the floods rose up, the winds lashed out. They all cut at that house, and it fell! And my, what a collapse!"

28. When Jesus finished speaking, the people were simply amazed at his ideas, for he was teaching them like he knew what he was talking about. He didn't sound like *their* preachers.

8.

1. As he came down from the hill, crowds of people flocked around him. And then here comes this guy in bad shape, begging and pleading, "Sir, if you really wanted to, you could heal me." Jesus put out his hand, hugged him, and said, "I *do* want to.

BE HEALED." And that quick his disease was gone! Then Jesus says to him, "Now look here, don't tell anybody about this, but go let the doctor examine you, and then you too start sharing like the Bible says, so as to be an example to others."

5. Well, when he got to Savannah a Jewish army captain came to him with an urgent message: "Sir, my boy is at home with a stroke and is in awful pain." Jesus says to him, "Then I'll come and cure him." But the army captain replies, "Sir, I'm not the kind of a man you'd want to associate with, so you just give the order, and my boy will be cured. You know, I myself am also a man with authority, having soldiers under my command. And I say to one,' Go there,' and he goes, and to another, 'Come here,' and he comes, and to my lieutenant, 'Do such-and-such,' and he does it." Upon hearing that, Jesus was simply amazed, and he said to those crowding around him, "I'm telling you the honest truth, never have I found such faith, not even among the good 'saved' church people. I want to tell you, many people will come from both North and South and sit down at the table with Peter, John, and Paul in the God Movement, but the 'saved' people will be dumped out into the black night, where there'll be a moaning and a groaning and a wringing of hands." So Jesus said to the captain, "You may go now. It'll turn out for you just as you believed it would." And within the hour his boy was cured.

14. Jesus went home with Rock, whose mother-in-law was in bed with a fever. He took her hand and the fever went away. So she got up and started waiting on him.

16. At sunset, they brought a lot of people who had devils, and by giving the order he purged them of their mean spirits and healed all who were in real bad shape. (This gave meaning to what Isaiah the prophet had said: "He himself took on our troubles and shared our sickness.")

18. Noticing the big crowd around him, Jesus planned to withdraw to the other side. And along the way this theologian said to him, "Doctor, I'll share your life, regardless of where it takes me!" Then Jesus said to him, "Foxes have dens, and the birds have nests, but the son of man has nowhere to hang his hat." Someone else—one of the students—said, "Sir, let me first take care of my family obligations."[4] But Jesus told him, "*You* live my life, and let the uncommitted care for the uncommitted."

23. He got in a boat and his students went with him. And wouldn't you know, such a terrific thunderstorm busted loose on the sea that you couldn't see the boat for the waves. Yet he was sleeping through it! They rushed to him and roused him. "Save us, sir! We're going down!" He said, "Why are you so scared, you baby-faiths?" Then he got up and told the wind and waves to cut it out, and everything got real still. The men were bug-eyed, saying, "What kind of guy is this, that even the wind and the waves listen to him?"

28. When he got to the other side, in Gadara County, he was met by two devil-possessed men coming out of the cemetery. They were such dangerous cats that nobody was able to travel that road. And you know, they screamed out, "What you got against us, you God's holy boy? Did you come here ahead of schedule to pick on us?" Now some distance from them a large herd of hogs was being fed. So the devils started begging him, "If you're going to dump us, send us among the herd of hogs." He told them, "Get moving." So they left and went among the hogs. And, would you believe it, the whole herd stampeded down the bank and into the sea, and died in the water! The herdsmen took off. They headed for the city and told everything, even what had happened to the devil-possessed fellows. And, man, the whole town turned out to gawk at Jesus. Then after they had seen him they begged him to please go away from their part of the country.

9.

1. Well, he got in a boat and sailed back across, and went to his hometown. And you know, they brought to him a paralyzed man lying on a stretcher. Jesus took note of their faith, and said to the paralyzed man, "Perk up, my boy. Your sins are being forgiven." Then some of the churchmen said, "This bird is talking *heresy!*" Jesus knew what was going on in their minds and said, "Why do you hold mean things in your hearts? Which is simpler, to say, 'Your sins are being forgiven' or 'Get up and walk'? But that you may have no doubt that the son of man has the right on the earth to forgive sins"—he then turned to the paralytic—"Get up now, pick up your stretcher, and run along home." And he got up and went home. A sense of awe came over the crowd when they saw it, and they applauded God for giving such authority to *human beings.*

9. Jesus left there and saw a man named Matthew sitting behind his desk at the Internal Revenue office. And he says to him, "Live my life." So Matthew quit his job and started living his life.

10. Well, one day when he was having dinner at home, a bunch of outsiders and unchurched people joined Jesus and his gang for the meal. Some good church people noticed this and said to his students, "How come your leader is eating with outsiders and unsaved people?" Jesus overheard it and replied, "It's not the healthy people who need the doctor, but the sick. Now you all run along and study over this verse: 'I want mercy and not worship.' For I didn't come to invite the 'good folks' but the 'unsaved.'"

14. Then John's followers came to him and asked, "How come we and the church members go to worship services all the time, but your students never attend?" Jesus asked them, "Does the wedding party hold a prayer meeting while the wedding is going on? Rather, when the ceremony is over and the bride and groom are gone, then they may have a worship service.

16. "Nobody ever uses new, unshrunk material to patch a dress that's been washed. For in shrinking, it will pull the old material and make a tear. Nor do people put new tubes in old, bald tires. If they do, the tires will blow out, and the tubes will be ruined and the tires will be torn up. But they put new tubes in new tires and both give good mileage."

18. As he was talking to them, a very important fellow came and humbly said, "My daughter just now passed away. So please come and put your hand on her, and she'll live." Then Jesus and his students got up and went with him. And you know, a lady who had been bleeding for twelve years came up behind him and touched his pants leg. She was thinking, "If only I touch his pants leg, I'll be healed." Jesus turned around and saw her, and said, "Cheer up, my daughter. Your faith has made you well." And from that hour on, the lady was normal.

23. Well, when Jesus got to the VIP's house and saw the people making the funeral arrangements and carrying on like mad, he said, "Y'all get out of here. The little girl isn't dead; she's just gone to sleep." They took it as a crude joke. But when the crowd was put outside, he took the girl's hand and raised her up. And news of this spread through the whole region.

27. As Jesus went along that way, two blind men followed him, shouting, "King Jesus, please do something to help us!" So when he went in the house and the blind men approached him, he asked them, "Do you really believe that I have the power to do this?" They answered, "Yes, sir!" Then he touched their eyes as he said, "Okay, let the thing you've believed happen to you." And their eyes were opened! Jesus looked real stern and said, "Don't you dare let a soul find out about this!" But they quick ran out and started spreading the news about him all over everywhere.

32. While they were going away, some folks brought to him a man who had a "dumb demon." So Jesus expelled the demon and the dumb man started talking. The crowds were astounded and said, "Nothing like this ever before happened in Georgia." But the religious people said, "He's expelling devils because he is in cahoots with the head devil."

35. Now Jesus went on a circuit of all the cities and villages, teaching in their churches, telling the good news of the Movement, and healing every disease and affliction. The sight of the crowds moved him to compassion for them, because they were as discouraged and disorganized as sheep without a shepherd. Then he said to his students, "There's a big crop, but not many workers. So beg the Harvest Master to recruit workers for his harvest."

10.

1. Jesus called together his twelve students and gave them control over mean spirits so as to expel them and to heal every kind of sickness and affliction. Now here are the names of the twelve "agents": first is Simon, who is called Rock, and Andy, his brother; Jim, Mr. Zebedee's boy, and his brother Jack; then Phil and Bart; Tom and Matt the revenuer; Jim Alphaeus and Tad; Simon the Rebel and Judas Iscariot, who turned him in.

5. Jesus held a briefing session and sent out the twelve. "Don't go after the people of the world," he said, "and don't enter the black ghetto. Instead go to the deluded racists of the nation.

As you travel, preach on the theme, 'THE GOD MOVEMENT IS HERE.' Heal the sick, arouse the insensitive, make the outcasts acceptable, expel devils. You received this power as a gift, so share it as a gift. Don't bother to take any money or travelers' checks or pocket change, no suitcase, no extra suit, no dress shoes, no toilet kit; for the worker is worth his upkeep. When you go to a city or town, discover who in it is receptive, and stay there till you're ready to leave. Upon entering a house, introduce yourselves. If the home is receptive, let your goodwill and concern rest upon it. If it is not, then hold on to your goodwill and concern. When somebody won't be friendly with you or pay attention to your message, leave that home or city and wash your hands of the whole shebang. I'm telling you a fact, Paris and Berlin will have it easier on the Judgment Day than that city.

16. "Listen, I'm sending you out like sheep surrounded by a pack of wolves. So be as alert as snakes and as pure as doves. Really keep your eyes peeled for people, for they'll trump up charges against you and even attack you in church. You'll be brought before legislative committees and high courts so as to make your witness before them and before the world in general. But when they take you to court, don't get the heebie-jeebies over your defense, because what you shall say will be given to you on the spot. For it won't be you that's talking, but the Spirit of your Father talking through you.

21. "Yes, a brother will betray his own brother to death and a father his own child, and children will rebel against parents and murder them. Furthermore, you'll be despised by everybody just because you are a true Christian. But the man who sticks it out to the end will be set free. So when they put the screws on you in one city, hightail it to the next, because I'm telling you the truth, you won't cover the Southern cities before the son of man overtakes you.

24. "A student is not above his teacher, or an employee above his boss. It would be pretty good if a student could just be equal with his teacher, or an employee with his boss. Well, if they slander the lord of the manor by calling him 'Dung-King,' what do you think they'll call his servants?

26. "But really, don't let them scare you. There is nothing under cover that won't be uncovered, or secret that won't be made public. What I'm making known to you at night, you proclaim at high noon, and what is whispered to you, you shout from the housetops. And don't be frightened by those who murder the body but can't kill the soul; rather, be afraid of the one who can make a hellish hash of both body and soul. Aren't two chicks sold for a quarter? Yet not one of them conks out apart from your Father. So y'all quit being scared; you people are worth more than a whole brooderful of chicks.

32. "Then whoever stands up with me before the world, I will stand up with him before my spiritual Father. But whoever lets me down before the world, I'll let him down before my spiritual Father.

34. "Don't get the idea that I came to set up peace all over the world. I didn't come to establish peace but strife. For I came to split a man from his father, a daughter from her mother, a bride from her mother-in-law. And a man's foes will be his own family. Anybody who puts his parents above me is not my man, and anybody who puts his children above me is not my man. And whoever does not accept his own lynching and share my life, is not my man. The person who hoards his life throws it away, and the one who abandons his life for my cause discovers it.

40. "The one who accepts you all accepts me, and the one who accepts me accepts him who sent me. He who entertains a man of God, aware that he is such, will get a man of God's pay; and he who entertains a man of justice, aware that he is such, will get a man of justice's pay. Anyone who gives only a glass of plain water to one of these little people, aware that he is my student, will by no means, I tell you, go unrewarded."

11.

1. And so, when Jesus got through briefing his band of twelve, he checked out of there to teach and preach in their cities.

2. When John, who was in the clink, heard the things the Leader was doing, he sent a message to him by his students. "Are you the Expected One," they asked, "or are we to wait for someone else?" Jesus replied, "Please go back and tell John what you are hearing and seeing—tell him the blind are seeing and the lame are walking, the lepers are getting well and the deaf are hearing, corpses are coming alive and the poor people are being told about the big doings. Tell him, too, that a man is wise not to be turned off by my thing."

7. As they left, Jesus began talking to the crowds about John: "What did you expect to see when you went out to the backwoods? A bamboo blown this way and that by the wind? Really, what *did* you expect to see when you went out? A man dressed up in his Sunday best? Listen, well-dressed people live in suburbs. Honestly now, why did you go out there? To see a man of God? Of course! And brother, I'm telling you, *what* a man of God! He's the one to whom this Scripture refers:

'I'm sending my agent to precede you;
He'll get everything ready for your coming.'

I tell you right now, John the Baptizer is the greatest man that's ever been born. *But, the tiniest baby in the God Movement is greater than he!* For ever since John the Baptizer started preaching until right now the God Movement has been infected with violence, and men of violence are taking it over. For until John's time all the prophets and the law spoke to this point. And if you are willing to admit it, John himself is the 'Elijah-to-come.' Now think that over!

16. "How shall I describe this generation? They are like kids playing in the streets and shouting at each other, 'We put on some rock-and-roll, but you wouldn't dance; so we put on some funeral music, but you wouldn't go into mourning.' For John offered a harsh, rugged life, and people say, 'The guy is nuts.' I, the son of man, offered laughter and joy, and people say, 'Look at that guy. He is a no-good bum who runs around with Communists and peaceniks!' So, if *intelligence* can be judged by its fruits, well—!"

20. Then he started lambasting the cities in which he had done most of his works, because they refused to re-order their lives. "It will be hell for you, Columbus; it will be hell for you, Albany; because if Dalton and Calhoun had seen as many mighty works as you have, they would have reshaped their lives right off the bat. But I'm giving it to you straight, Dalton and Calhoun will have it a lot easier on Judgment Day than you will. And you, Savannah, do you think you'll be praised to the skies? You'll be sent to hell! Because if the mighty works which have been done in you had happened in Sodom, it would be standing till this very day. But I'm giving it to you straight, it will be easier on Sodom on Judgment Day than on you."

25. About that time Jesus said, "I fully agree with you, Father, Ruler of things both spiritual and material, that you didn't let the bright boys and the experts in on these matters, but made them clear to the 'babies.' Indeed, O Father, this is the way it seemed best to you.

27. "My Father has left everything up to me. No one truly knows the Son except the Father, and no one truly knows the Father except the Son and whoever else the Son wishes to introduce to him.

28. "Come to me, all of you who are frustrated and have had a bellyful, and I will give you zest. Get in the harness with me and let me teach you, for I am trained and have a cooperative spirit, and you will find zest for your lives. For my harness is practical, and my assignment is joyful."

12.

1. Along about then Jesus went through a wheat field on a Sunday. His students were hungry, so they started picking some heads, rubbing out the grains with their hands, and eating them. Some church members saw it and said, "Look, your students are doing something they shouldn't on Sunday." He answered, "Haven't you ever read what David and his companions did when they were hungry? How he went into the church house and ate the communion bread, which neither he nor his companions were entitled to—only the ministers were? Or haven't you read in the Bible how ministers work hard at church on Sunday but are not blamed for it? But let me set you straight: what's here is more important than a church building! If you had but understood what this means—'It's compassion I want, and not worship'— you wouldn't have jumped down the throat of innocent people. For the son of man has authority over 'Sunday.'"

9. He went on from there and entered their church building, and a man with a paralyzed hand was there. Trying to hang something on Jesus, they asked, "Is it legal to heal on a Sunday?" He said to them, "Is there a single man among you who, if he should own a sheep and it should fall in a hole on a Sunday, would not get hold of it and pull it out? Well, isn't a *man* worth more than a *sheep*? So it's perfectly all right to act beautifully on a Sunday." Then he said to the man, "Stretch out your hand." And he stretched it out and, sure enough, it was normal, just like the other one. But the church members went out and held a conference on how they might do him in. Jesus was aware of it and checked out of there. Even so, a lot of people stayed on his trail, and he made them all well. He pled with them to please not make his whereabouts known. (All of this gave meaning to what Isaiah the prophet said:

> "See, my man whom I selected,
> My loved one of whom I'm so proud.
> I will put my breath in him,
> And he will shout for justice for the black people.
> He won't wrangle and hassle,
> Nor make soapbox speeches.
> He won't even wring a chicken's neck,
> Or cut off a puppy's tail,
> Until he has won out in the fight for justice.
> His name will inspire hope in the black people.")

22. Then a possessed man who was blind and dumb was brought to him. He healed the man so he could talk and see. The whole crowd thought it was simply beautiful, and they said, "*Isn't this our Man?*" But the church members overheard it and replied, "Why, this guy couldn't run off mean spirits unless Dung-King, the head Confuser, gave him a hand." Jesus read their minds and said, "Any nation that fights itself will go to pot, and any city or business that beats itself over the head won't survive. So if

Dung-King runs off Dung-King, he's fighting himself. How, then, will his business survive? Okay, so I'm driving out mean spirits with Dung-King's help. Now with whose help are *your* disciples driving them out? They, then, convict you. But, if I, by God's Spirit, am driving out mean spirits, then the God Movement is squarely confronting you. Look, how can someone break into an armed man's house and rob him without first overpowering the armed man? Then he can make off with the loot. The man who is not with me is against me, and if he doesn't help me he hurts me.

31. "So let me level with you: Any sin and disgrace will be forgiven men except the disgracing of the Spirit. If anybody gives the son of man a black eye, it will be forgiven, but whoever gives the Holy Spirit a black eye will not be forgiven, either nor or in the future. So, either make the tree true and its fruit true, or make the tree wild and its fruit wild. For the fruit from a tree identifies it.

34. "You sons of snakes, how can you say good things when you are wicked, since the tongue is powered by the overflow from the heart? The good man produces good deeds from the good things stored in his heart, while the mean person produces mean deeds from the mean things stored in his heart. It's a fact that at the time of testing men will account for every unguarded word they utter. For you will be cleared or convicted by what you affirm or deny."

38. Then some preachers and church members got together and said, "Professor, we want you to give us a demonstration." He answered, "A mean and wicked society demands a 'demonstration,' but none will be given to it except Preacher Jonah's 'demonstration.' For just as Jonah spent three days and nights in the monster's belly, so will the son of man spend three days and nights in the heart of the earth. In the Judgment the Ninevites will testify against this society and will convict it, because they reshaped their lives around Jonah's message, and now a greater one than Jonah is here. In the Judgment, the Queen of the South will testify against this society and convict it, because she came from the ends of the earth to hear Solomon's wisdom and now a greater one than Solomon is here.

43. "When a filthy spirit comes out of a man, he wanders through unwatered areas looking for a home. Finding none, he says, 'I'll go back to my house that I left.' He does so, and finds it vacant, cleaned up, and painted. Then he goes and rounds up seven other spirits more wicked than himself, and they all move in and live there. So the man is worse off at the end than he was at the beginning. The same will also be true of this wicked society."

46. While he was still talking to the people, somebody told him, "Your mother and your brothers are standing outside trying to have a word with you." He said to the man who told him this, "Who is my mother, and who are my brothers?" And he stretched out his hand toward his students and said, "There are my mother and my brothers. The man who does the will of my spiritual Father is my brother and sister and mother."

13.

1. One day Jesus left the house and sat down on the seashore. Such a big crowd gathered around him that he got into a boat and sat down while the people stood on the beach. He told them many Comparisons: "One time a farmer went out to plant. As he did so, some of the seeds fell on the path, and the birds came along and gobbled them up. Others fell on rocky places where the soil was shallow. Because they weren't planted deep they came up right away, but not having a deep root they withered when the hot sun hit them. Still others fell among the weeds, which grew up and choked them out. But others fell on good dirt and matured, some multiplying a hundred times, some sixty, and some thirty. Now please let *that* soak in."

10. Then the students came and asked him, "Why are you giving it to them in Comparisons?"

"Because," he said, "they have not been let in on the secrets of the God Movement like you have. When a man has them, he'll be given more and will have plenty; when a person doesn't have them, he'll lose even what he has. The reason, then, that I give it to them in Comparisons is that they look without seeing and listen without hearing or catching on. This passage from Isaiah applies to them:

> 'They strain their ears and never catch on;
> For the hearts of these people are hard,
> And their ears are dull,
> And their eyes are dim.
> Otherwise, their eyes might see,
> And their ears might hear,
> And their hearts might understand,
> And they might turn around,
> And I'll make them well.'

But you, you should be truly thankful that your eyes see and your ears hear. For indeed many sincere and just men of God would have given their eyeteeth to see and hear what you are experiencing, but they never had the chance. So you all pay attention now to the planting-farmer Comparison: When someone hears the Movement idea and doesn't latch on to it, the evil one comes along and makes off with what was planted in his mind. This is the 'path' seed. The 'rocky places' seed is the one who listens to the idea and gets gung-ho about it, but having no inner depth he hangs on for a while until hardship and persecution for the cause come along, and then he washes out. The 'seed in the weeds' is the one who hears the idea, but is overcome by the distractions of life and the love of money before it can bear fruit. The 'good dirt' seed is the one who hears the idea and latches on to it, and it yields possibly a hundredfold, or sixty, or thirty."

24. Then he laid before them another Comparison: "The God Movement is like a man who planted certified seed in his field. Then after everybody had gone to bed, his enemy came and overplanted the wheat with zizania. When it all came up and started to grow, the zizania was clearly present. The farmer's fieldhands came to him and said, 'Sir, didn't you plant certified seed in your field? Then how come it's got zizania in it?' He replied, 'An enemy did that!' The fieldhands asked, 'Do you want us to go and chop it out?' The farmer said, 'No, because you might dig up the wheat with the zizania. Let them both grow until harvesttime. Then I'll say to the harvest workers, "Gather all the zizania first and pile it up for burning, and then harvest the wheat and put it in my barn."'"

31. He set still another Comparison before them: "The God Movement is like a mustard seed which a man planted in his garden. While it's the smallest seed there is, yet when it is full grown it is one of the largest plants; in fact, it becomes a bush big enough for birds to build their nests in."

33. He told them another Comparison: "The God Movement is like yeast which a woman puts in a triple recipe until the whole batch rises."

34. Jesus taught the crowds all these things with Comparisons. Actually he wasn't teaching them at all except by Comparisons. (The word of the prophet might be applied to him:

"I will break forth with Comparisons;
I'll spotlight things that have been taboo since
creation.")

36. Then he left the crowds and went into the house. His students gathered around him and said, "Please unravel for us the Comparison of the field of zizania." He answered, "The farmer who planted the certified seed is the son of man; the field is the world; the certified seed are the people who do God's will; the zizania are the people u-ho do the will of the evil one; the enemy is the Confuser; the harvest is the fruition of the era; and the harvesters are God's messengers. So, just as the zizania was piled and burned, that's the way it will be at the fruition of the era. The son of man will send out his messengers and they'll collect everything in his Movement that's offensive and all the criminals, and they'll burn them in a roaring furnace. In there, they'll be howling and snapping their teeth. Then the just will shine like the sun in their Father's Movement. Now let *that* percolate through.

44. "The God Movement is like a man finding a treasure buried in a field. He covers it over again, and then with great excitement he sells all he owns and buys that field.

45. "Also, the God Movement is like a jeweler looking for special pearls. When he finds a super-duper one, he goes and unloads his whole stock and buys that pearl.

47. "Still again, the God Movement is like a fishing net that's thrown into a lake and catches all kinds of creatures; when it's full, then they pull it up on the bank and separate the catch, putting the good stuff in tubs and throwing away the bad. That's the way it will be at the fruition of the era. The messenger will go out and cull the unjust from the just and throw them into a roaring furnace. In there, they'll be howling and snapping their teeth. Now is all this clear to you?"

They said, "Absolutely!" He told them, "Then every minister who has completed the God Movement course is like a quarter master who comes up with both new and old things from his warehouse."

53. Well, when Jesus got through with all these Comparisons, he pulled out of there and went to his hometown. He started teaching in the church there, and really bowled them over. They said, "Where did that guy get all this learning and big-league stuff? Ain't this the carpenter's boy? Ain't his mama named Mary and his brothers Jim and Joe and Simon and Jody? And his sisters, don't they all live around here? Then how did he come by all this?" So they got plenty miffed at him, and he said, "A true prophet is never appreciated by his own hometown and by his kinfolks." Because of their disrespect, then, he did nothing really significant there.

14.

1. About that time Governor Herod heard the news of Jesus, and he said to his cronies, "I'll bet it's John the Baptizer. He has been raised from the dead, and that's why he can do such amazing things." For Herod had arrested John, chained him, and kept him in jail after John had told him, "It isn't right for you to take Herodias, your brother's wife."

5. Herod was anxious to kill him, but he was scared to because the people regarded John as a man of God. Well, at Herod's birthday party, Herodias' daughter danced for him and delighted him so much that he swore he would give her anything in the world she asked for. Having been put up to it by her mother, she said, "Give me, here on a platter, *the head of John the Baptizer.*" Hearing this, the Governor wanted to kick himself for having made such a rash promise in public, but he went ahead and gave orders to have John beheaded in the jail. Then John's head was brought in on a platter and presented to the young lady, and she took it to her mama. John's friends went and got his body and buried it; then they got in touch with Jesus and told him about it.

13. When Jesus heard it, he left there in a boat to go to a quiet place where he could be alone. But the crowds from the cities heard about it and flocked after him on foot. When he went ashore and saw what a crowd it was, he was deeply moved by them, and he healed their sick ones. Toward the close of the day, his students came and said, "This is a deserted place, and it's already getting late. Dismiss the people so they can go to town and buy something to eat." Jesus told them, "They don't need to leave; you all feed them." They said, "But we have nothing on hand—except five boxes of crackers and two cans of sardines." He said, "Okay, bring them here." So he told the people to sit down on the grass, and then he took the five boxes of crackers and two cans of sardines. Lifting his eyes toward the skies, he said a blessing and gave the food to his students, who distributed it among the people. Everybody ate and had plenty, and there were twelve basketsful of leftovers. The number fed was about five thousand men, not counting the women and children.

22. Shortly afterwards he urged his students to get into the boat and go on over ahead of him while he dismissed the crowds. When he had dismissed them, he went into the mountain to pray privately. As the sun set, he was there by himself.

By this time the boat was some distance from shore. The wind was against them and the waves were giving them fits. Late at night Jesus came to them walking on the lake. His students saw him walking on the lake and it scared the daylights out of them. "It's a ha'nt!" they screamed. But Jesus quickly called to them, "Y'all take it easy. It's just me; don't be so scared!" Rock called out, "Sir, if it *is* you, tell *me* to come walking on the water to you!" Jesus said, "Come on!" Rock clambered out of the boat and started walking on the water, heading for Jesus. But when the wind hit him he got scared stiff and, beginning to sink, he yelled, "Save me, sir!" At once Jesus put out his hand and grabbed him. "Why did you lose your nerve, baby-faith?" Jesus asked. They climbed back in the boat, and the wind died down. Those in the boat humbled themselves before him and said, "You are surely God's Man!"

34. They sailed over and came to the Geneva area. As soon as the people around there recognized him, they sent word to the outlying neighborhoods and everyone brought all their ailing ones to him. They asked him to let them touch his shirttail, and all who touched it were completely healed.

15.

1. Then some laymen and ministers from Atlanta approached him and asked, "How come your followers go against the customs of religious people by not saying grace before meals?" He answered, "Well, how come you yourselves break God's law with your customs? For God says 'Cherish your father and mother,' and 'He who renounces his father or mother shall be put to death.' But *you* teach that 'if a man tells his father or his mother, "I've donated to the church all that I had set aside for you," he has not deserted his father or his mother.' You completely set aside God's Word with a custom like that. You phonies, Isaiah was surely talking about you when he said,

'These people cherish me with their mouths,
But their hearts are miles from me.
Their worship of me isn't worth a tinker's dam;
Their teachings are man-made rules.'"

10. He called out to the crowd and said, "Y'all listen now and get this straight: It isn't what goes *into* a man's mouth but what comes *out of* it that debases him." Then the students went up to him and said, "Did you realize that when the church members heard what you said they were pretty riled up?" He answered, "Every plant that was not set out by my spiritual Father will be pulled up by the roots. Let them be. They are blind guides of the blind. If a blind man leads a blind man, they'll *both* fall in a ditch." Rock spoke up, "Bust open the Comparison for us." Jesus said, "Are y'all that dumb too? Don't you understand that whatever goes into the mouth passes *into* the belly and then becomes dung? But what comes *out of* the mouth springs from the heart and *that* debases a man. But to eat food that hasn't been blessed doesn't debase anybody."

21. Jesus left there and arrived in the region of Dalton and Calhoun. Then a black woman from those parts came up and started pleading with him, "Please, sir, help me! My daughter is badly demon possessed." But he didn't answer her a word. Then his students came along and advised him, "Tell her to scram, because she's making too much noise!" He replied, "I was sent only to needy white people." But she came and humbled herself before him and said, "Sir, please help me!" He answered, "It isn't right to take the bread from the children and throw it to the puppies." She said, "Yes, but even so, sir, the puppies *do* get the *scraps* from their masters' table." Then Jesus said to her, "Ma'am, you've got a *lot* of faith. You may have whatever you want." And her daughter was healed from that instant.

29. Well, Jesus left there and went over around Lake Lanier, and he climbed up a hill and stayed there. Then large crowds gathered around him. They had with them the crippled and deformed, the blind, the dumb and many others, and they rushed to put them at Jesus' feet. When he healed them, the crowd just couldn't get over the fact that they were seeing dumb people talking, deformed ones made normal, crippled ones walking, and blind ones seeing. And they praised the God of Jesus' people.

32. Now Jesus summoned his students and told them, "I am deeply concerned for the crowd, because they've already been with me for three days and they've run out of food. I hate to let them leave hungry; they might pass out along the way."

The students asked, "But where will we find food enough out here in the country for all this crowd?"

Jesus said, "Well, how much have you got?"

"Seven loaves of bread," they said, "and a few fish." So after he told the people to sit down on the ground, he took the seven loaves and the fish, gave thanks, broke them into pieces, and distributed them among the students, who then served the people. Everybody ate and had plenty, and they had seven basketsful of leftovers. Four thousand men, not counting women and children, were fed. He dismissed the crowds, got in a boat and went into the Magadan area.

16.

1. Some Protestants and Catholics got together to test him, and they asked him to show them his spiritual credentials. He replied, "At dusk you say, 'The sky is red; it'll be fair,' and at dawn you say, 'The sky is red and darkening; it'll rain today.' You are able to read the clouds but not the signs of the times. A mean and faithless generation asks a sign from me, and the only sign it will get is that of Jonah." So he turned his back on them and left.

5. When the students went across with him, they forgot to take bread. Jesus said to them, "Now let me warn you to stay away from the yeast of the Protestants and Catholics." They tried to figure that one out themselves, and decided he had said it because they had no bread. When Jesus found out about it, he said, "Why was it, baby-faiths, that you were hashing over the fact that you have no bread? Haven't you caught on yet? Don't you remember the five boxes of crackers of the five thousand and how many basketsful of leftovers you had ? Or the seven loaves of the four thousand, and how many basketsful you had left over? Well, why can't you get it through your heads that I wasn't speaking to you about bread ? Rather, I told you to stay away from the *yeast* of the Protestants and Catholics." Then it soaked in that he had not warned of the bread yeast, but of the *teachings* of the Protestants and Catholics.

13. When Jesus came into the region of Augusta, he asked his students, "Who do people think the son of man is?"

They said, "Some say John the Baptizer, others say Elijah, and still others, Jeremiah or one of the famous preachers."

"But you, who do you think I am?" he asked.

Simon the Rock spoke right up and said, "You are the Leader, the Living God's Man."

"You are beautiful, Simon Johnson!" exclaimed Jesus. "This isn't human reasoning, but divine revelation. And I want to tell you, you are Rock, and on this rock[5] I will build my fellowship, and the doors of death will not hold out against it. I will give to you the keys of the God Movement, and whatever you bind in the physical realm shall have been bound in the spiritual realm, and whatever you loose in the physical realm shall have been loosed in the spiritual realm." Then he strongly warned them to tell no one that he was the Leader.

21. From then on Leader Jesus began to make clear to his students that he had to go to Atlanta and to go through terrible things at the hands of the leading church people—to be killed, and three days later to be raised! But Rock collared him and began to take him to task. "Not on your life, sir," he said, "Be dadblamed if this will ever happen to you." Jesus whirled on Rock and said, "Get away from here, you devil; you are gumming up the works for me, because you're not following God's ideas but human reasoning!" Jesus then said to his students, "If a man wants to walk my way, he must abandon self, accept his lynching, and share my life. For the person who aims to save his life will lose it, and the one who loses his life for my cause will find it. What's a man's advantage if in getting the whole world he loses his life? Indeed, what shall a man trade in his life for?

27. "The Leader and his spiritual band will shortly come, with the full backing of his Father, and then he will assign every man on the basis of his activity. I give you my word, some of those standing right here won't die before they see the Leader heading his Movement."

17.

1. Six days later Jesus withdrew into a very high mountain, and he took with him only Rock and Jim and Jim's brother, Jack. And before their very eyes his form changed—his face lit up like the sun and his clothing became as bright as light. Then they saw Moses and Elijah talking with him. So Rock spoke up and said to Jesus, "Sir, it sure is wonderful that we are here. If you say so, I'll build three chapels on this spot—one for you, one for Moses, and one for Elijah." He had hardly gotten it out of his mouth when a brilliant cloud enveloped them, and from the cloud came a voice, "This is my dear Son, who greatly pleases me; do what he tells you." When the students heard that they fell to the ground, scared out of their wits. Jesus came over to them, picked them up, and said, "Y'all get up and don't be so scared." They looked up at him, and saw he was by himself.

9. As they made their way down the mountain, Jesus warned them, "Don't tell a soul about the vision until the son of man is raised from the dead." Then the students asked, "Well, how come the professors say that Elijah has to come first?" He replied, "Elijah indeed does come and get everything in order; in fact, Elijah has already come, and nobody recognized him, so they treated him like anybody else. They'll do that and worse to the son of man." The students then realized that he was referring to John the Baptizer.

14. As they approached the crowd, a man came running up and said, "Sir, please do something about my son, because he is crazy and is in bad shape. Many times he falls into the fire and frequently into the water. I brought him to your students, but they couldn't heal him."

Jesus answered, "You bankrupt, misguided people! How much longer must I be with you? How much longer must I go to bat for you? Bring him here to me." Then Jesus chewed out the demon and it left, and the boy was completely well from that time on.

When Jesus was alone, the students approached him and asked, "How come *we* couldn't get that demon out?"

"Because of your baby faith," he said. "It's an absolute fact that if you have faith like a mustard seed, you will say to this hill, 'Move from here to there,' and it will be moved. Nothing will be too big for you."

22. While they were touring Georgia, Jesus said to them, "The son of man will soon be turned in to the authorities, and they'll kill him—and on the third day he'll be raised." This nearly tore their hearts out.

24. During their stay in Savannah, some church fundraisers came to Rock and asked, "Does your leader make donations to the church?" Rock replied, "Yeah." When Rock went inside, Jesus took it up with him. "What do you think, Simon? Where does the government get its funds? From taxes on itself or from nongovernment sources?" Rock said, "Why, from nongovernment sources." Jesus answered, "So the government, then, is tax-exempt![6] But, to keep from upsetting them, go down to the lake and throw your line in, open the mouth of the first fish you catch, and you'll find a ten-dollar bill. Take that and make a donation for both you and me."

18.

1. Along about then, his students raised this question with Jesus: "Who, now, is the top man in the God Movement?" He called a little child to him and said, "It's a straight fact that unless you turn around and become like little children, you won't have a ghost of a chance in the God Movement. So the person who brings himself as low as this kid will be the top man in the God Movement. And whoever recognizes one such youngster in my name recognizes me. Anybody who trips up one of these little ones who trust me would be better off if a grinding rock were draped around his neck and he were drowned in the bottom of the sea. The world is in an awful mess because of its traps. They do have to be, but it will be hell for the man who sets them.

8. "If your hand or foot gets caught in a trap, cut it off and throw it away. For it is better to be alive, maimed or crippled, than to have both hands or both feet and be thrown into the bag of destruction. And if your eye makes you fall into a trap, cut it out and throw it away. For it is better to be alive, one-eyed, than to have both eyes and be roasted over the pit. Be careful that you don't look down your nose at a single one of these little people, for it's a sober fact that their spiritual envoys are in constant contact with my spiritual Father.

12. "How do you see it? If a man owns a hundred sheep and one of them strays off, won't he leave the ninety-nine in the pasture and go look for the stray? And when he finds it, I'm sure that he's more proud of it than of the ninety-nine that didn't stray. That's exactly the way it is with your spiritual Father. He doesn't want a single one of these little people to be abandoned.

15. "If your brother does you wrong, go talk it out privately between the two of you. If he sees your point, you've won your brother. But if he won't see your side of it, take one or two others, since every fact, in order to stand, must have two or three witnesses. If he will pay them no mind, bring it up before the church. If he won't pay attention to them, chalk him up as a hopeless case.

18. "I give you my word that whatever you bind in the physical realm shall have been bound in the spiritual realm, and whatever you loose in the physical realm shall have been loosed in the spiritual realm. Again I want to tell you that if two of you in the physical realm covenant together about any matter of concern, it will be acted on for them by my spiritual Father. For where two or three are banded together as Christians, I am present with them."

21. Then Rock sidled up and asked, "Sir, how often should I forgive my brother when he keeps doing me wrong? Seven times?"

"I wouldn't say seven times," Jesus replied, "but *seventy times seven!* That's why the God Movement is like a big businessman who wanted to settle the accounts of his customers. As he started to do so, one customer came in who owed a bill of more than ten thousand dollars. He had nothing to pay on the account, so the businessman told the sheriff to put up for sale everything the guy had and apply it to the debt. But the fellow did a song and dance. 'Please give me some more time and I'll pay every cent!' he begged. The businessman was touched by the guy's pitiful pleas, so he let him go and marked off the debt. Then that same guy went out and found a man who owed him a hundred dollars. Grabbing him around the neck, he choked him and said, 'Pay me that money you owe.'

'Please give me a little more time,' the man begged, 'and I'll pay every cent.' But he refused and, instead, he swore out a warrant for him. When the little man's friends found out about it, they were really upset, so they went and told the big business-man all that had happened. Then the big businessman sent for the guy who had owed him the huge debt and said to him, 'You low-down bum! I marked off all that debt for you because you begged me to. Shouldn't you, then, have been kind to that little man just as I was kind to you?' Still hot under the collar, he turned the fellow over to the law to be thrown into the clink until every last dime of the debt had been paid. And my spiritual Father will treat you along the same lines unless every single one of you forgives your brother from your heart."

19.

1. So, when Jesus got through with these lessons, he left north Georgia and went into that section of south Georgia around the Chattahoochee. Great crowds flocked after him, and he healed them there.

3. Then some church members, trying to get something on him, came and asked, "Under what circumstances is it all right for a man to divorce his wife?"

He replied, "Haven't you ever read how at the beginning the Creator made them man and woman, and said, 'To preserve this, a man shall not give first place to his father and mother but shall be fully committed to his woman, and the two of them shall become one bundle of humanity'? So they cease to be two people—they are one. Therefore, let no man split up what God has teamed together."

"Then why," they asked, "did Moses rule that a man could divorce a woman by giving her a signed statement that she was free?"

"Moses let you divorce your wives," he replied, "because of your own bullheadedness. But it was not that way to start with. So I'm telling you that anybody who divorces his wife, except for sleeping with another man, and then marries someone else, is committing adultery."

10. The students remarked, "If that's the situation between a man and his wife, maybe they shouldn't marry at all."

"What I've just said," he answered, "does not apply to everybody, but to certain people. For example, some are born without sexual capacity, others have been robbed of it by their fellow men, and still others have sacrificed it for the cause of the God Movement. Let whoever the shoe fits wear it."

13. Then they brought some children to him, that he might put his arms around them and pray for them. The students bawled out the people who had brought them. But Jesus told them, "You let those kids come to me, and don't you dare get in their way, for they are the material of the God Movement!" And he put his arms around them and then left there.

16. One day a fellow came to him and said, "Doctor, what is the good that I should follow in order to get spiritual life?"

"Why are you inquiring about 'the good'?" Jesus asked. "'The good' is one. But if you want to come into the life, abide by the rules."

The fellow said, "Which ones?"

Jesus answered, "Why, the ones that say, 'Don't murder, don't sleep with someone you're not married to, don't steal, don't lie, take care of your father and mother, and love your neighbor as yourself.'"

"I've kept them all," cried the young man. "Why am I still flunking?"

"If you want to be a mature man," Jesus said, "go, sell your stuff, give it to the poor—you will be spiritually rich—and then come share my life." When the young fellow heard that bit, he walked away crying, because he had quite a pile. Jesus said to his students, "I'm telling you a fact; a rich man finds it extremely difficult to come into the God Movement. I say it again, a pig can go through a knothole easier than a rich man can get into the God Movement."

Upon hearing this, the students were completely flabbergasted. "Who can make the grade?" they asked.

Jesus looked straight at them and said, "Humanly speaking, this is impossible, but with God anything can happen."

27. Then Rock popped off, "Look at us! We have thrown everything overboard and shared your life, so how will we come out?"

Jesus answered, "Let me tell you something: When the new order is ushered in and the son of man takes office, then you all who have shared my life will be appointed to the twelve posts of the cabinet and will be responsible for the functioning of the new government. And anybody who has thrown overboard houses or brothers or sisters or fathers or mothers or children or farms for the sake of my cause will get them back a hundred times over, and will also receive spiritual life. But many on top will be on the bottom and many on the bottom will be on top.

20.

1. "The God Movement is like a farmer who went out early in the morning to hire some field workers. Having settled on a wage of ten dollars a day, he sent them into the cotton field. Then about nine he went to town and saw others standing around idle. So he said to them, 'Y'all go on out to the fields, and I'll pay you what's right.' And they went. He did the same thing about noon, and again around three. Then about an hour before quitting time, he saw some others just hanging around. 'Why have y'all been knocking around here all day doing nothing?' he asked. 'Because nobody has hired us,' they answered. 'Okay, then y'all can go out to the cotton fields too,' he said. At the end of the day the farmer said to his field boss, 'Call the workers and pay them off, starting with those who came last and continuing to the first ones.' Well, those who came an hour before quitting time were called up and were each paid ten dollars. Now those who got there first thing in the morning supposed that they would get much more, but when they were paid off, they too got ten dollars. At that, they raised a squawk against the farmer. 'These latecomers didn't put in but one hour, and you've done the same by them as you did by us who stood in the hot sun and the scorching wind.' But the farmer said to one of them, 'Listen, buddy, I haven't mistreated you. Didn't you and I settle on ten dollars a day? Now pick up your pay and run along. I'm determined to give this last fellow exactly the same as you. Isn't it okay for me to do as I please with what's mine? Or are you bellyaching simply because I've been generous?' That's the way it is: Those on the bottom will be on top, and those on top will be on the bottom."

17. As Jesus was planning to go to Atlanta, he called the twelve aside and said to them along the way, "Look, we're headed for Atlanta, and the son of man will be handed over to the officials and they will pass the death sentence on him. They'll turn him over to the mob to have fun poked at him, to be flogged, and to be lynched. And on the third day he will be made alive!"

20. Then the mother of the Zebedee boys came to him with her two, greeted him, and said she would like to ask a favor of him. "What do you want?" he asked.

"Please arrange it," she said, "so that one of these two sons of mine might be your first vice-president in the Movement and the other your second vice-president."

Jesus answered, "Y'all don't realize what you're asking. Are you able to drink the cup that I'm about to drink?"

They said, "We sure are!"

"All right," he said, "you'll drink my cup, but to make one of you my first vice-president and the other my second vice-president is not up to me. These positions are for those who have been prepared for them by my Father." When the other ten got wind of this, they were plenty sore at the two brothers. So Jesus called them all together and said, "You are aware that the world's big shots lord it over people and the high brass throws their weight around. But it's not that way with you. If one of you wants to be a head man, let him be your general flunky. Your example is the son of man himself, who didn't come to be served, but to serve and to give his life for the life of the masses."

29. As they left Griffin a big crowd went with him. Two blind men were sitting beside the road, and when they heard that Jesus was passing by, they yelled, "Please, Mr. David's son, have mercy on us!" But the crowd chewed them out and told them to shut up. Instead, they yelled even louder, "Please, Mr. David's son, have mercy on us!"

So Jesus stopped and called out to them, "What do you want me to do for you?"

"Our eyes, sir," they said, "make them see!" Jesus' heart melted, and he touched their eyes. Right away they saw, and they went along with him.

21.

1. As he neared Atlanta he came to Peach Orchard Hill, outside Hampton. There he sent two students ahead, with these instructions: "Go into the next town, and as soon as you enter it you will find a donkey tied up and a mule with her. Untie them and bring them to me. And if anybody questions you, just say, 'Their owner needs them,' and he'll let you have them right away." (This happened to give meaning to the words of the prophet:

> "Spread the word in the capital:
> Look, your king is entering you,
> An humble man riding a donkey,
> Riding a mule, a lowly work animal.")

6. So the students left, and did exactly as Jesus had told them. They brought the donkey and the mule, put their own coats on them, and Jesus jumped on. Many in the crowd made a carpet of their coats while other plaited twigs cut from trees and lined the road with them. Huge crowds of people, some going in front of him and some following him, were cheering loudly:

"Hurrah for our Leader!
Long Live the Lord's Man!
Hurrah for God Almighty!"

When he entered Atlanta, the whole city was all shook up. "Who is this guy?" they asked. And the crowd replied, "He is a man of God—Jesus, from Valdosta, Georgia."

12. Then Jesus went into First Church, pitched out the whole finance committee, tore up the investment and endowment records, and scrapped the long-range expansion plans. "My house shall be known for its commitment to God," he shouted, "but you have turned it into a religious racket!" And the blind people and the broken people gathered around him in the church, and he made them well. But when the district superintendents and the ministers saw the fantastic things he was doing, and the young people loudly cheering in the church, "Hurrah for our Leader," they blew their stacks. "Don't you hear what these kids are screaming?" they growled. "Yes, indeed," Jesus exclaimed, "and haven't you ever read that 'I'll weave a hymn of praise from the babblings of babies and the cries of kids'?" He walked away, left the city and spent the night in Jonesboro.

18. Upon returning to the city early next morning, he was hungry, so when he saw a lone peach tree beside the road, he went over to it. But he found that it had nothing on it but leaves. He said to it, "You'll never in this world bear fruit." And quick as a wink it wilted. This astounding sight stood the students on their ear. "How about that! The peach tree wilted in a wink!" But Jesus told them, "Listen here, if you hold on to your faith and don't chicken out, you'll do not only the peach tree thing, but even if you tell this hill, 'Get up and jump in the lake,' it will happen; in fact, when you put your faith into action, you get *anything* you pray for."

23. Returning to the church, he was approached during a teaching session by some ministers and elders who asked, "What right do you have to do these things? Who gave you this permission?"

Jesus replied, "All right, I'll ask you just one question, and if you answer it, then I'll tell you where I got permission to do these things. John's baptism, was it divine or human?"

They conferred with one another, saying, "If we tell him 'divine,' then he'll ask us, 'So why didn't you accept it?' If we say 'human,' we're scared of John's crowd, because they all regard him as a man of God." So they told Jesus, "We really don't know."

"Okay," he said, "then I won't tell you where I got the authority for my actions. But give me a reading on this: A man had two boys. He went to the older one and said, 'My boy, go work in the orchard today.' He said, 'Will do, Pop,' but he never did. Then he went to the younger one and told him the same thing. But the boy said, 'I won't go.' Afterwards he felt like a heel, and did go. Which of the two obeyed his father?"

"Why, the last one," they said.

"And I'm telling you the honest truth," Jesus said, "that the hippies and the whores are taking the lead over you into the God Movement. For John confronted you with the way of justice, and you didn't buy it. But the hippies and the whores bought it, and you knew it. Even this, though, didn't make you feel like a heel afterwards and go buy it yourselves.

33. "Listen to another Comparison. Once there was a farmer who set out a peach orchard, built a fence around it, bought some equipment, and put up a packing shed. Then he rented it to some sharecroppers and left. When peach-picking time came, he sent his workers to the croppers to get his share of the fruit. But the croppers took his workers and beat one of them, killed another, and stoned the other. So he tried again, this time sending more important workers than before, but the croppers treated them the same way. Finally he sent his son, thinking that surely they would respect *him.* But when the croppers saw the son they got together and said, 'Hey, there's the old man's boy. Let's kill this cat and take over his estate!' So they grabbed him and dragged him out of the orchard and murdered him. Now, when the owner of the orchard comes, what will he do to those croppers?"

They answered, "Why, he'll tear those bastards to bits, and let out the orchard to croppers who'll give him his share of the fruit at harvesttime."

Jesus asked them, "Haven't you ever read in the Bible: 'The stone which the craftsmen rejected was selected as the cornerstone. This was done by the owner, and is an amazing sight for us'? Now that's why I'm telling you that the God Movement will be taken out of your hands and turned over to people who will be productive. (And the person who falls on this stone will be splattered, but whoever it falls on will be pulverized.)" The ministers and church people listened to his Comparisons, and were aware that they were aimed at them. They were dying to arrest him, but feared the crowd, who regarded him as a man of God.

22.

1. Jesus continued the conversation by speaking to them with Comparisons. "The God Movement is like a governor who gave a big dinner for his party chairman. He told his secretaries to invite the prominent dignitaries, but they refused to accept. So he told his secretaries to try again. 'Tell them,' he said: "'The banquet is all arranged for—the steer has been butchered and the hogs barbecued. Y'all come on to the dinner.'" But they couldn't have cared less. One left to go out to his farm; another went to his store. The rest of them taunted and insulted the secretaries. At that, the governor had a duck fit, and ordered the names of the scoundrels to be struck from the list of his friends. Then he said to his secretaries, 'Plans for the banquet are all made, but the people I invited aren't fit to come. So go to the various precincts, and whoever you find there, invite them to the banquet.' Well, they went to the precincts and brought in everybody they could find, good and bad. The banquet hall was filled with guests, and the governor went in to greet them. There he saw a guy sitting at the table who looked and smelled like he had just come in from his farm. The governor said to him, 'Hey, buddy, how did you get in here, looking and smelling like that?' He just clammed up. Then the governor said to the waiters. 'Tie the bum up and throw him in the back alley.' Outside there'll be yelling and screaming, for the big ones were invited but the little ones got in."

15. Then the good church members got together and hatched a plot to trap him in something he said. So they sent him a committee with some FBI men. "Doctor," they said, "we know that you are a straight shooter, and that you tell God's way like it is. And it doesn't matter to you who you're talking to, because you pay no attention to a man's standing. Now please give us your opinion on this matter: Should one pay Federal taxes or not?"

Catching on to their trick, Jesus asked, "Why are you putting me in a bind, you phonies? Show me a dollar." They brought him a dollar, and he said, "Whose engraving is on it?"

They said, "The government's."

"All right, then," he replied, "give the government's things to the government and God's things to God."

When they heard that, it bowled them over and they laid off him and left.

23. The same day some liberals, who say there's no life after death, gathered around him and put this question to him: "Doctor, the Old Testament says that if a man dies without having any children, his brother shall marry the widow and have children by her for his brother. Now, there were seven brothers among us. The first one married and died, and since he had no children, he left his wife to his brother. The same thing happened with the second and the third, on through the seventh. Finally the woman died. Now then, in the hereafter, which of the seven will she belong to, since all of them were married to her?"

29. Jesus retorted, "You're off the beam, understanding neither the Scriptures nor God's power. In the hereafter people are not married, but are in the Spirit, like angels. But regarding the afterlife, haven't you ever read how God told you, 'I am the God of Abraham, the God of Isaac, and the God of Jacob'? He is not, then, the God of the dead but of the living." And as the crowds listened, they were spellbound by his teaching.

34. When the church members found out that he had cooked the liberals' goose, they ganged up on him, and one of their bright boys, trying to get Jesus over a barrel, asked, "Doctor, what is the most important commandment in the Bible?" Jesus said, "'You shall love your Lord God with your whole heart and with your whole soul and with your whole mind.' This is the greatest and most important commandment. Next to it is this one: 'You shall love your fellow man as yourself.' The whole Bible hinges on these two."

41. The next time the church members met, Jesus asked *them* a question: "What do you think about the Leader? Whose son is he?"

They answered, "David's."

"Then why did David refer to him as his spiritual master when he said, 'The Master said to my master, "Sit at my right hand while I bring all who oppose you under your rule"'? If then David calls him 'master,' how can he be his son?" Not a soul could answer him one word, and from that day on nobody had the guts to put another question to him.

23.

1. Then Jesus opened up on the crowds and to his students: "The theologians and the preachers plant their feet in the Bible; therefore, listen to all they tell you and live by it. But don't you act like them, because they are forever talking and never doing. They sack up heavy loads and strap them on men's backs, but they themselves won't lift a little finger to carry them. Their every action is for show. They strut in their robes and display their degrees. They love the seats at the speaker's table at banquets, and the pulpit chairs in the churches, and the backslapping at civic clubs. They like to be called 'Reverend.' But don't let yourselves be called 'Reverend,' for you have but one pastor and you all are brothers. And don't call a human being 'father,' for you have but one spiritual Father; neither be called 'doctor,' for you have but one Doctor—the Leader. Your top man shall be your houseboy. The fellow who promotes himself will get bumped, and whoever bumps himself will get promoted.

13. "It will be hell for you, theologians and preachers— phonies, because you lock men out of the God Movement. You not only won't enter yourselves, but you slam the door on those who do.[7] It will be hell for you, theologians and preachers—phonies, because you send missionaries around the world to make one convert, and when you win him you make him double the devil's son that you are. It will be hell for you, you blind leaders who say, 'If somebody pledges by the sanctuary,[8] he may renege, but if he pledges by the *gold* in the sanctuary, he has to pay.' You blind nitwits, which is more important, the gold or the sanctuary that houses the gold? You also say, 'If somebody pledges by the altar table he may renege, but if he pledges by the offering on the altar table, he must pay.' Moles, which is more important, the offering or the altar table on which it is laid? So anybody who pledges by the altar table pledges by it and everything on it. And anybody who pledges by the sanctuary pledges by it and by its Occupant. And the one who pledges by heaven, pledges by God's throne and by him who sits on it.

23. "It will be hell for you, theologians and preachers—phonies, because you tithe your pennies, nickels, and dimes, and pass up the more important things in the Bible, such as justice, sharing, and integrity. You ought to practice these without neglecting those. You addlebrained leaders, you fence in a flea and let your horse escape. You save your trading stamps and throw your groceries in the garbage.

25. "It will be hell for you, theologians and preachers—phonies, because you trim the lawn and paint the house, but inside there is nothing but greed and selfishness. Blind ecclesiastic, first clean up the inside of the house, that the outside too might be neat.

27. "It will be hell for you, theologians and preachers—phonies, because you resemble landscaped slaughterhouses, which look beautiful on the outside, but inside are full of blood and entrails. That's exactly the way you are. Outwardly you impress people as men of justice, but inside you are full of phoniness and fraud.

29. "It will be hell for you, theologians and preachers—phonies, because you build churches and name them after the saints, and you set up orders to honor the faithful. You say, 'If we had been alive in those days we wouldn't have joined our forefathers in murdering the men of God.' By this you do admit that you are *descendants* of prophet-killers. You yourselves live up to your forefathers' reputation! Copperheads, sons of snakes, how can you escape hell's damnation? Now look, I'm sending to you men of God and competent teachers and ministers. Some of them you'll hound to death and lynch, and some of them you'll castigate in your churches and pester from city to city. Over you, then, hangs the guilt for the murder of every innocent man since time began, from the murder of innocent Abel to the murder of Zack Bronson, who was shot between the church and the parsonage. I'm telling it like it is, *all* of this will hang over this generation.

37. "O Atlanta, Atlanta! Killer of prophets and assassinator of statesmen, many times I wanted to draw your people together as a hen snuggles her biddies under her wings, and you would have none of it. All right, your affairs are in your own hands, but I'll tell you this, you won't see me around again until you're crying out, 'Please God, send us some spiritual leadership.'"

24.

1. As Jesus was leaving First Church, his students gathered around and made comments to him about the church's beautiful architecture. He responded, "You see all this layout, don't you? I've got news for you: not one piece of marble will be left upon another without being torn down."

3. Later, as he was sitting on Peach Orchard Hill, his students came to him privately and said, "Please tell us when this will happen, and what will be the signal for your *coup* and the finishing off of the regime."

4. "Don't let anybody kid you," he told them, "for there will be many people buzzing around calling themselves Christians and saying, '*I'm* the Leader,' and they'll dupe a lot of folks. But you'll soon hear of strife and sounds of strife. Don't get upset, for that's the way it has to be, but that's not really the end. Race will rise against race, and nation against nation. There will be disasters and shakeups in various places. All these things are but the first labor pains of the new order. Then they will tar and feather you and kill you, and you'll be hated by just about everybody— simply because you are my people. At that time many will be washed out and they'll squeal on one another and hate one other. Many ministerial quacks will come along and hoodwink the crowds. And because of the increased rioting, many people's goodwill will be cooled off. But the one who sticks with it to the finish will be saved. And this good news of the Movement will be spread throughout the world as an established fact for mankind; then the finish will come.

15. "So, when you see the tyrannical foreign power, spoken of by Daniel the prophet, occupying the government (you know who I mean), then the people of the country should take to the hills; the guy at the office must not go home to pack up, and the farmer in the field must not go back for his Sunday clothes. It will be hell for the pregnant and for those who are nursing babies in those days. Just pray that this won't happen during winter or on a holiday, for there will be great suffering, the like of which has never been known since the beginning of time until now, nor ever will be. And had not its duration been shortened on account of the remnant, not a soul would come through it alive. If anyone at that time tells you, 'Here are the Christians over here,' or 'Here we are right here,' pay them no attention. For fake messiahs and phony preachers will get up all over the place and put on big shows and crusades so as to bamboozle, if they can, even the true believers. Now listen, I'm forewarning you. Therefore, if they tell you, 'Ah, he is at the retreat center,' don't go out there; or if they say, 'Oh, he is in our meetings,' don't be sucked in. The *coup* of the son of man will be just like a bolt of lightning springing from the east and flashing across the sky to the west. Wherever there's something dead, buzzards will be circling.

29. "Immediately after the anguish of those days, the sun will be turned into darkness, the moon will lose its lustre, the stars will fall from heaven, and the cycle of the spheres will be broken. Then the signal of the son of man will appear in the sky. After that, all the nations of the earth will cry out, and they'll see the son of man riding the clouds of the sky with great pomp and majesty. And he will send his messengers with a terrific trumpet to assemble his true believers from North and South and East and West.

32. "Now consider this Comparison with a peach tree: When its buds swell and it puts out leaves, you know that summer is on its way. All right, by the same token, when you see all this taking place, you know that here it is on your doorsteps. I assure you that before this generation is gone, things will be popping. Land and sky will cease to be, but my words will stand to eternity.

36. "Nobody—not even the angels in heaven or the Son, only the Father—knows about the *final* day and hour. The *coup* of the son of man will be similar to Noah's situation. During the days just before the flood, it was 'business as usual' for everybody right up till the day Noah went into the ark. They were unconvinced until the flood came and swept everything away. The son of man's *coup* will be like that. When it happens, two brothers will be in the field; one will be caught up and one will be left plowing. Two sisters will be fixing dinner; one will be caught up and one will be left cooking. So stay on your toes, because you can never tell what day your master will come. And keep this in mind: if the homeowner knew what time the thief was coming, he would wait up for him and not allow his house to be robbed. By the same token, you too be on the alert, because the son of man might arrive at a time when you're not expecting it.

45. "Well then, who is the loyal and efficient worker whose boss will put him in charge of his payroll to see that everyone is promptly and accurately paid? Happy is that worker who, when his boss shows up, is hard at it. I assure you he'll give him one promotion after another. But if that guy is a stinker and tells himself, 'My boss will be late this morning,' and starts throwing his weight around and abusing his co-workers, and then goes out for a snack and a few beers, sure as anything his boss will show up just when he is least expected and will tear him apart and fire him. That will give him something to moan and groan about.

25.

1. "The God Movement, then, may be compared to ten young ladies who got their lanterns and went out to join a wedding party. Five of them were giddy-witted and five were cool. The giddy-wits took their lanterns but no oil, while the cool ones took extra oil for their lanterns. The wedding procession was late in coming, so they all started nodding and napping. Along about midnight someone yelled, 'Hey, the procession is coming! Jump up and join it!' So all the girls woke up and got their lanterns in order. The giddy-wits said to the cool gals, 'Our lanterns are going out; please let us have some of your oil.' But the smart ones said, 'We can't; there isn't enough for both of us.

You'd better go to the store and buy some for yourselves.' While they were gone to the store, the procession came and those who were all set went along into the ballroom, and the doors were closed. Later on, the other girls came running and said, 'Mister, Mister, let us in!' But he replied, 'I don't recognize you.' So keep your eyes open, because you never know the day or hour.

14. "It's like a businessman who was leaving town for a long time and called in his assistants and turned over his investments to them. He made one responsible for about five hundred thousand dollars, another two hundred thousand, and another a hundred thousand—according to each one's ability—and then he left town. Right away the man with the five hundred grand got to work and made five hundred more. The man with the two hundred grand did the same and made another two hundred. But the guy with the hundred G's went and rented a safe-deposit box and put his boss' money in it. After a long time the boss returned and called his assistants together for an accounting. The one with the five hundred thousand brought his other five hundred thousand and said, 'Sir, you let me have five hundred grand; look, I've made another five hundred.' The boss said, 'Splendid, you good and responsible worker! You were diligent with the smaller sum; I'll entrust you with a larger one. You'll be a partner in my business.' Then the one with the two hundred G's came and said, 'Sir, you let me have two hundred thousand; look, I've made another two hundred.' The boss said, 'Splendid, you good and responsible worker! You were diligent with the smaller sum, I'll entrust you with a larger one. You'll be a partner in my business.' Well, the hundred-grand man came up and said, 'Sir, I know you are a hard-nosed man, squeezing pennies you haven't yet made and expecting a profit before the ink has dried. I was plain scared to take any chances, so I rented a safe-deposit box and put your money in it. Look, you've got every cent.' But his boss replied, 'You sorry, ornery bum! You knew that I squeeze pennies I haven't yet made, and expect profits before the ink dries. Then you should have turned my money over to the bank so that upon my return I would get back at least my principal with interest. So then, y'all take the money away from him and give it to the one with the million. For it will be given to everyone who has the stuff, and he'll have plenty, but the man who doesn't have the stuff will have even what he has taken away from him. Now as for this useless critter, throw him in the back alley. That'll give him something to moan and groan about.'

31. "When the son of man starts his revolution with all his band around him, then he will assume authority. And all the nations will be assembled before him, and he will sort them out, like a farmer separating his cows from his hogs, penning the cows on the right and the hogs on the left. Then the Leader of the Movement will say to those on his right, 'Come, you pride of my Father, share in the Movement that was set up for you since creation; for I was hungry and you shared your food with me; I was thirsty and you shared your water with me; I was a stranger and you welcomed me, ragged and you clothed me, sick and you nursed me; I was in jail, and you stood by me.' Then the people of justice will answer, 'Sir, when did we see you hungry and share our food, or thirsty and share our water? When did we see you a stranger and welcome you, or ragged and clothe you? When did we see you sick or in jail, and stand by you?' And the Leader of the Movement will reply, 'When you did it to one of these humblest brothers of mine, you did it to me.'

41. "Then he will say to those on his left, 'Get away from me, you fallen skunks, and into the flaming hell reserved for the Confuser and his crowd. For I was hungry and you shared nothing with me; I was thirsty and you gave me no water; I was a stranger and you didn't welcome me, ragged and you didn't clothe me, sick and in jail, and you didn't stand by me.' Then these too will ask, 'Sir, when did we see you hungry or thirsty or a stranger or ragged or sick or in jail, and do nothing about your needs?' Then he'll answer, 'When you failed one of these humblest people you failed me.' These will take an awful beating, while the just ones will have the joy of living."

26.

1. When Jesus concluded these lessons, he said to his students, "You all realize that the annual convention is only two days away, and the son of man will be taken out and lynched."

3. Then the executives and board members got together at the office of the chairman, whose name was Caiaphas. The purpose of the meeting was to find a way to take Jesus on the sly and do him in. They said, "Not at the convention, because it might start a riot among the people."

6. When Jesus was at the home of Simon the wino in Jonesboro, a woman with a bottle of very high-priced perfume came and dabbed it on him while he was eating. When the students noticed it, they boiled over: "What's going on? Why waste this when it could be sold for a neat sum and used for the poor?" Jesus got wind of it and said, "Why are you bitching at the lady? She has done something beautiful for me. You have poor people with you all the time, but you don't have *me* all the time. By putting this perfume on my body she has prepared me for burial. I assure you that wherever the gospel is preached she will be remembered for what she has done."

14. At this time, one of the twelve, Judas Iscariot, went to the executives and said, "How much will you give me to deliver him to you?" They set the price on him at thirty silvers.[9] From then on, Judas was looking for an opportunity to deliver him.

17. On the first day of the convention, the students came to Jesus and said, "Where shall we arrange to have the annual banquet?" He said, "Go into the city and tell Mr. So-an'-So, 'The Professor says, "I'm just about ready. I plan to have the banquet with my students at your place."'" The students did as Jesus directed, and made preparations for the banquet.

20. That night Jesus sat down at the table with the twelve, and as they were eating he said, "I'm convinced that one of you will turn me in." They were simply horrified at this, and each one began asking, "You're not talking about me, are you, sir?" He replied, "The person who will turn me in is one who served himself from the same plate I did. Indeed the son of man is going the same way the Scriptures said he would, but it will be hell for that fellow who turns him in. It would have been better for him if he had never been born." Then Judas, who actually did turn him in, asked, "You're not talking about me, are you, Doctor?" Jesus said to him, "You're right."

26. During the banquet Jesus took a loaf, and having blessed it he broke it and gave it to the students. "Take it and eat," he said; "this is my body." He also took the cup, and after the thanksgiving prayer he gave it to them and said, "Y'all drink out of it; this is my blood. It is being shed for many so as to write the Constitution of the Clean State. I'm telling you that I am drinking no more of this 'fruit of the vine' until that day when I drink new wine with you in my Father's Movement."

30. Well, they sang something and went out to Peach Orchard Hill. Then Jesus said to them, "On this very night every last one of you will chicken out on me, for it is written, 'I'll slug the shepherd, and the flock of sheep will be scattered all over.' But after I'm raised, I'll go on ahead of you into Alabama." Rock spoke right up, "Even if the whole bunch chickens out on you, I myself will never in this world chicken out on you." Jesus said to him, "Let me tell you something: Tonight—before the rooster crows at dawn—you'll disown me three times." Rock told him, "I don't care if I have to *die* for you, I positively will *not* disown you." And that's what they all said.

36. Then Jesus went with them to a spot called McMath's Mill, and he said to his students, "Y'all please stay here while I go over yonder to pray." Taking with him Rock and the two Zebedee boys, he began to show his heartbreak and weariness of soul. "I'm so heavy-hearted that it's about to crush the life out of me," he told them; "please stay here and sweat it through with me." And he went a little farther, and fell on his face praying, "O my Father, if it's possible, please relieve me of this agony! But I want *you* to decide it, not me."

40. He went back to the students and found them dozing. So he said to Rock, "How about that! Weren't you fellows able to stick with me for even an hour? Get with it and start praying so that you don't get into a bind! Even though the heart is right, the will is weak." He left again and prayed a second time, "O my Father, if it's impossible to relieve me of this agony without my going through with it, then let your will be done." Then he returned, and found them dozing again, for their eyes were as heavy as lead. He let them be, and went back again and prayed a third time, saying the same thing over. He then came to his students and told them, "Y'all sleep on a while and relax; the time for the son of man to be turned over to wicked people is close. . . . Hey, get up, let's go! The man turning me in is here now!"

47. Even as he was saying it, Judas, one of the twelve, came up, and with him was a mob sent out by the power establishment and armed with guns and clubs. Now Jesus' informer had arranged to give the mob a signal: "He'll be the one I kiss[10]; nab him." So he walked right up to Jesus and said, "Hello Doctor!" And he kissed him.[11] Jesus said to him, "O buddy, what have you arrived at?" Then they came and grabbed Jesus and arrested him. Right then one of those with Jesus reached in his pocket and pulled out a switchblade. He slashed at the archbishop's lackey, and sliced off his ear. Then Jesus shouted at him, "Put that switchblade back in your pocket! People who use violence are destroyed by it. Or are you thinking that I can't call on my Father and get him to instantly send me more than a dozen battalions of angels? But then, how would the writings that it must turn out this way have any meaning?"

55. At the same time Jesus said to the mob, "So you have come out here armed with guns and clubs to take me as though I were a seditionist? Day after day I taught openly at the church and you didn't lay hands on me. But this whole thing has happened so that the writings of the men of God might have meaning." Then all the students left him in the lurch and got out of there fast.

57. The gang that got Jesus took him to Caiaphas, the archbishop, where the ministers and elders were gathered. Keeping his distance, Rock trailed him as far as the archbishop's backyard, and went inside and sat with the servants to see how it would turn out. Now the executives and the whole council were trying to bring a false charge against Jesus that would justify putting him to death, but from all the liars who testified, they couldn't make a case. Finally two of them testified, "This fellow said, 'I can tear down God's house and build it up during three days.'" The archbishop faced him and asked, "Can you make any answer to these men's accusations?" Jesus was silent. The archbishop said to him, "I put you under oath to the living God to tell us if you are God's appointed Leader—God's Man." Jesus replied, "You are right. But I have news for you all: From now on you'll be seeing the son of man exercising his power and riding on the clouds of the sky."

65. Then the archbishop unzipped his robe and exploded, "He's mocking God! Why do we need any more witnesses? Just look! Y'all heard the impudent mockery. What do you think?" They responded, "Guilty! Let him die!" Then they spit in his face and whacked him over the head. Those beating him said, "Tell us, Mister Leader, which one socked you?"

69. Rock was still sitting outside in the yard. A young girl came up to him and said, "Say, you too were with Jesus the Georgian." He flatly denied it right in front of everybody, "I don't know what you're talking about." When he went over to the gate, another girl saw him and said to the others standing there, "This fellow was with Jesus." This time he flatly denied it in stronger terms, "I'll be damned if I even know the guy." A little later, some who were standing around turned to Rock and said, "It's for sure that you are one of them, because your accent gives you away." Well, at that Rock began to cut the blue and use some nautical language. ". . . I don't know the man! " he said. Right then the rooster crowed. Rock remembered how Jesus had told him, "Before the rooster crows you'll disown me three times." And he went out and cried like a baby.

27.

1. At daybreak all the executive board deliberated on how to put Jesus to death. They beat him up real good, and took him over and turned him in to Governor Pilate.

3. When Judas, who had squealed on him, realized that Jesus had been condemned, he broke down and took the thirty silvers back to the archbishop and elders, and said, "I've done wrong; I've ratted on an innocent man." They replied, "What's that to us? You tend to it." And he slammed the money down in the church and left, and hanged himself. The church officers picked up the money, but felt it wouldn't be proper to put it in the church treasury, since it was tainted with blood. So they passed a motion to buy the Potter place with it, as a cemetery for outsiders. That's why to this day that field is called "The Blood Plot." And this gave meaning to something Jeremiah the prophet said, "And they took the thirty silvers, the price they felt was a fair price for a man from Georgia, and used them for the Potter place, as the Lord instructed me."

11. Jesus now appeared before the governor. "Are you the Head of the Church?" the governor inquired. "You are right," replied Jesus. But when the church officers tried to hang something on him, he made no defense. Pilate then said to him, "Are you admitting their charges against you?" But Jesus did not defend himself on a single count, which greatly surprised the governor.

15. Now each year at the annual convention the governor had a practice of pardoning some prisoner the people demanded. Right then there was a very famous prisoner in jail named Jesus Daddy-boy.[12] So when they assembled, Pilate asked them, "Who shall I pardon for you—Jesus Daddy-boy or Jesus the Father's Anointed?" (Pilate detected that they had arrested Jesus out of pure meanness.)

19. While the trial was going on, Pilate's wife sent word to him: "Don't get tangled up with that honest man, because I had a horrible nightmare about him last night."

20. Well, the leaders of the council pressured the mob to ask for Daddy-boy to be released and Jesus to be condemned. So when the governor asked them, "Which of the two do you want me to pardon for you?" they shouted, "Daddy-boy!"

Pilate asked them, "Then what shall I do with Jesus, God's Anointed?" They all yelled, "Kill him!"

"But what's his crime?"

They screamed even louder, "Kill him!"

24. When Pilate saw that he wasn't getting anywhere, but that a big stir was brewing, he got some water and washed off his hands publicly. "I am clearing myself of this man's blood," he said; "you yourselves are responsible." The whole crowd answered back, "His blood will be on us and on our children!" Then Pilate pardoned Daddy-boy, and he had Jesus beaten and turned over to them to string up.

27. The governor's troopers then took Jesus into the barracks and passed the word around among all the boys. They stripped him naked, dressed him up in a black clerical robe, and made a dog collar out of burlap. They put a Bible in his hand, came by and shook hands with him and wisecracked, "Good morning, Reverend, Leader of the Faithful." And they spit on him, and took the Bible and clobbered him over the head with it. When they got through deviling him, they took off the clerical garb and put his own clothes back on him, and led him away to string him up. On the way they found an outsider named Simon, and they made him tote Jesus' cross.

33. Well, they got to a place called "Skull." They offered him a drink of wine mixed with a drug, but when he tasted it, he wouldn't drink it.

They nailed him to the cross.

They rolled dice to see who would get his clothes.

They sat around watching him there.

Over his head they put a copy of the charge against him. It read: "This is Jesus, the Leader of the Faithful."

Two revolutionaries were nailed up with him, one on his right and one on his left.

People passed by him and razzed him. They wagged their heads and said, "Hey, you who can tear down God's house and build it up in three days, get yourself out of this pickle. If you're God's Man, bust loose from the cross!" The bishops and preachers and elders acted the same way. They said, "He got others out of their bind but he can't get out of his own. He is the Leader of the Faithful; let him break loose from the cross now and *we* will be his faithful ones. He set his heart on God; now if God wants him, let him rescue him. After all, he did say, 'I am God's Man.'"

The revolutionaries who were crucified with him taunted him with the same kind of stuff.

45. From noon till three a darkness settled over the whole place. About three o'clock Jesus groaned loudly: "*Eli, Eli, lama sabachthani?*" which means, "O my God, O my God, why have you left me here?"

When some of those standing around him heard that, they said, "Listen, the man is calling on Elijah!" One of them ran real quick and got a sponge, soaked it in wine, and put it on a stick and held it to his mouth. The rest said, "Don't do that! Let's see if Elijah will come and rescue him."

50. Jesus again gave a loud cry. Then he died.

And you know, the big curtain in the sanctuary of First Church was torn in two, from top to bottom.

And the earth shook, and the rocks were split.

Graves were laid open, and many bodies of dedicated dead people were made alive. They came out of the graves, and after

Jesus' resurrection they went into Atlanta, and made themselves known to many people.

54. Now when the captain and his buddies who were keeping an eye on Jesus saw the earthquake and the happenings, they were scared out of their wits. "No doubt about it," they said, "this guy really was God's Man."

55. Some distance away a number of ladies, who had followed Jesus from Alabama to wait on him, were watching it all. Among them were Mary, "that girl from Magdala," and Mary, the mother of Jim and Joe, and the mother of the Zebedee boys.

57. Late that afternoon a well-to-do man arrived, a Jesus convert named Joseph, from the white suburb of Sylvan Hills. He went to Pilate and requested Jesus' body; then Pilate ordered it to be granted. So Joseph took the body and wrapped it in a clean sheet, put it in his new burial vault, which he had cut out of a rock, rolled a huge stone over the entrance, and left. Mary, "that girl from Magdala," and the other Mary were sitting there opposite the vault.

62. On the next day, Saturday, the church leaders met with Pilate and said, "Sir, we just happened to remember that while that crook was alive he said, 'In three days I'll be raised.' Give the order, then, for the vault to be guarded through the third day, to keep his followers from coming and stealing him and then telling the people, 'He was raised from the dead.' *That* trick would be worse than any previous ones." Pilate told them, "Okay, you may have a guard. Go and make it as secure as you know how." They left and put an official seal on the stone, and secured the grave with a guard.

28.

1. As the Sabbath ended, at the crack of dawn on Sunday, Mary, "that girl from Magdala," and the other Mary came to visit the vault. And you know, a big commotion happened. An angel of the Lord came down out of the sky and went and rolled away the stone, and sat down on top of it. His face was like lightning and his clothes were white as snow. The guards were so shook up that they looked like corpses. But the angel said to the ladies, "Don't y'all be scared one bit, because I know that you're looking for Jesus who was lynched. He isn't here. He was raised just as he told you. Come here; look at the place where he was lying, then go right away and tell his students that he has been raised from the dead. And one thing more: he is going on ahead of you into Alabama; you'll see him there. Now, I've made it clear to you."

8. So they left the vault and, filled with both fear and great excitement, they ran like mad to tell his students. And what do you know, *Jesus* met them. He said, "Howdy." They went to him and hugged his feet and him. Then Jesus told them, "Y'all quit being so scared. Run along now and tell my brothers that they should go over into Alabama, and they'll see me there."

11. After the women left, some of the guards, you know, went into town and related to the bishops everything that had happened. They met with the elders and passed a motion that the soldiers be given a large bribe, with these instructions: "Tell people that his students came at night while we were sleeping, and stole him. If the governor gets wind of this, we'll fix it with him and arrange it so you won't have a worry in the world." The soldiers took the bribe and did exactly as they were instructed. And to this very day that's the rumor circulated by the good white folks.

16. Well, the eleven students traveled to Alabama, to the mountain which Jesus had selected for them. When they saw him they accepted him as their Lord, but some couldn't make up their minds. Jesus came over to them and said, "Every right to rule in both the spiritual and physical realms has been given to me. As you travel, then, make students of all races and initiate them into the family of the Father and of the Son and of the Holy Spirit. Teach them to live by all that I outlined for you. And you know, I am right in there with you—all the time—until the last inning."

Notes for Matthew

[1] Or Joshua, which means "Deliverer" or "Savior."

[2] The argument here seems to be that sex, a God-given function like the eye or the hand, may become the focal point of moral infection and cause the destruction of the whole personality. Under these conditions, as with a badly infected eye or hand, it is better to give up sex than to let it ruin one's whole life.

[3] That is, with one eye on one thing, the other on something else.

[4] Literally, "let me give priority to burying my father." This does not mean that the father was dead—or even ill. To "bury" someone meant to fulfill all obligations up to and including the final one of burial.

[5] A literal translation of the Greek goes like this: "You are *petros* [rock masculine gender] and on this *petra* [rock, feminine gender] I will build . . . ." Obviously the masculine form refers to the disciple. The feminine cannot refer to Rock himself, but possibly to his "revelation" (feminine gender in the Greek) that Jesus is the Living God's Man.

[6] The argument here is that since Jesus and his group *are* "the government," or the church, they technically would be exempt from the obligation of contributing to the church.

[7] Some reliable manuscripts add verse 14: "It will be hell for you, theologians and preachers—phonies, because you make a killing on slum property and polish your public image by holding evangelistic meetings. You'll get the judgment book thrown at you."

[8] It appears from this that in Jesus' day ecclesiastical real estate could be used for private collateral.

[9] The exact amount is not clear from the Greek text. It could have been anywhere from thirty silver coins, a relatively small amount, to thirty silver talents, a small fortune.

[10] The Greek word used here is an untranslatable one, about like "shake hands with."

[11] Unlike the previous word for "kiss," this one is deeply emotional and conveys much love and tenderness. It is used only three other times in the New Testament. The woman of sin, whose tears wet Jesus' feet, dried them with her hair and "kept kissing his feet" (Luke 7:38). When the prodigal son returned home, the waiting father ran to meet him and "fell on his neck and kept on kissing him" (Luke 15:20). And when Paul summoned his beloved Ephesian brothers to Miletus to bid them final farewell, telling them that they would never see his face again, "everybody started crying their eyeballs out as they put their arms around Paul and kissed him and kissed him" (Acts 20:37 CPV). Apparently, then, Judas' kiss of farewell was no less emotional. The "sign," which was intended to be a superficial kiss of greeting, turned into a tear filled kiss of intense love. Perhaps, like the woman of sin, Judas too, wet his master with his tears.

[12] Literally, "Son-of-a-father."

John

1.

1. When time began, the Idea already was. The Idea was at home with God, and the Idea and God were one. This same Idea was at home with God when time began. Through him the universe was made, and apart from him not one thing came to be. In him was life, and the life was humanity's light. And the light shines on in the darkness, and the darkness never quenched it.

6. A man arose—sent from God—whose name was John. This man came forward as a witness, to testify for the light, so that people might be convinced by him. He wasn't the light himself, but a witness for the light. The true light, which enlightens every man, was entering the world. In the world he was, and the world was made by him, and the world ignored him. He came into the things he had made, and the people whom he loved turned their backs on him. However, to those who did let him in—who lived up to his name—he gave the right to be God's children. Such children were not fathered by bloody sacrifices, nor by a moment of lust, nor within wedlock, but by God himself.

14. Well, the Idea became a man and moved in with us. We looked him in the face—the face of an only son whose father is full of kindness and integrity.

15. As John preached, he had this to say about him: "This is who I meant when I said, 'The one coming behind me has gotten ahead of me, because he was here before I was.'"

16. All of us got one favor after another from his overflowing abundance. Moses gave us rules; Jesus the Leader gave us kindness and integrity.

John

18. While no one has ever actually seen God, the only One—the Father's dearest One—has revealed him.

19. Here is John's testimony when the good white folks of Atlanta sent a committee of preachers and deacons to ask him what he considered himself. He admitted right off the bat and stood his ground, publicly asserting, "I am *not* the Leader."

So they asked him, "Well, what are you, then? Are you an Elijah?"

"No, I'm not," he replied.

"Are you 'The Prophet'?"

"Nope."

"Look, we've got to make a report to those who appointed us," they said. "What are you? What claims are you making for yourself?"

"I am what Isaiah the prophet said—a voice crying in the wild, 'Straighten out the Lord's road.'"

24. Since they had been appointed by the denomination, they inquired, "Well, if you aren't the Leader, nor an Elijah, nor 'The Prophet,' then why are you initiating members?" John told them, "Indeed I am initiating—in water. But right in your midst is standing one who you fellows don't recognize. He follows me, but I myself am not fit to shine his shoes." All this happened in Jonesboro, across the Chattahoochee, where John was immersing.

29. Next day, John saw Jesus coming to him. "Y'all look! There's God's Lamb, the world's sin-bearer! That's the one I was talking about when I said, 'A man is coming behind me who has gotten ahead of me, because he was there before I was.' Even I was not sure of him, but that he might be introduced to the nation, I began a pre-enrollment in water."

32. John testified further: "I saw the Spirit, descending like a dove from the sky, and lighting on him. And even I was not sure about him, but he who sent me to dip in water also told me, 'The one upon whom you see the Spirit descending and lighting will be the one who immerses you in Holy Spirit.' Well, I saw it, and I have emphatically stated that *this* is God's Man."

35. The following day John was standing with two of his converts, and when he saw Jesus walking around, he again cried out, "Y'all look! There's God's Lamb!" The two converts, upon hearing John say that, started following Jesus. Jesus noticed that they were following him, and he turned around and asked, "What's on your mind?" They asked, "Reverend, where are you staying?" He told them, "Come and see." So they went and saw where he was staying, and they visited with him that whole day until about four o'clock.

40. Andy, the brother of Simon (Rock), was one of the two who got the word from John and followed Jesus. The first thing he did was to find his own brother and tell him, "We have discovered the *Christ-os*" (or, to put it in English, "God's Leader"). He took him to Jesus. Jesus sized him up and said, "You are Simon Johnson;[1] you'll be nicknamed *Petros*" (or, in English, "Rock").

43. A day later, Jesus wanted to leave for north Georgia. He ran across Phil, who was from Albany, the hometown of the Johnson brothers, and said to him, "Join me."

Phil looked up Nat and told him, "We have discovered the One the Bible talks about! His name is Jesus (Joseph's boy), and he's from Valdosta!"

Nat said, "From Valdosta! Could anybody worth his salt come from there?"

Phil said, "Come and take a look."

Jesus saw Nat approaching him and commented, "Look! There's a real white man! There's nothing phony about him."

Nat asked, "Where did you hear about me ?"

"I saw you," Jesus replied, "before Phil talked with you under the muscadine vine."

"Reverend," answered Nat, "you are God's Man; you are the nation's Leader!"

"Are you convinced merely because I told you that I saw you under the muscadine vine?" Jesus asked. "You'll see a whole lot more than that. In fact, I want to tell y'all that you'll see the sky busted open and God's angels climbing up and climbing down on the son of man!"

2.

1. On Tuesday there was a wedding celebration at Canton north Georgia, and Jesus' mother went. He and his students ere also invited to the celebration. Well, the wine started running low, and Jesus' mother told him, "That's all the wine they've got." Jesus said, "What are you and I to do about it, ma'am? . . . I'm not quite ready. . . ." His mother turned to the servants, "Help him in any way he needs you."

6. Now there were six stone water jars put there for carrying out the Old Testament rules for keeping things clean. Each held two or three buckets of water. He told the servants, "Fill e crocks with water," and they filled them up to the brim. Then Jesus said, "*Now* let your bucket² down and draw up some for the emcee." They fetched it. When the emcee tasted the water-become-wine, he didn't know where it came from, though the servants who had bucketed it up knew. The emcee called the groom and said, "People always put on the good wine first, and when everybody is pretty well tanked up, they bring out the cheap wine. But you have saved the best wine till last." Jesus did this first sign in Canton, Georgia, and showed his credentials. And his students put their faith in him.

12. Later, he and his mother, his brothers and his students went down to Savannah and stayed there a short while. Well, it was about time for the annual convention, so Jesus went to Atlanta. At the convention headquarters at First Church he found preachers politicking, and businessmen wheeling and dealing, and exhibits all over the place. So he got a long-handled fly swatter and a broom and began clearing out the crowd and wrecking the merchandise booths. "Get out of here with all this stuff!" he shouted. "Quit making a racket of my Father's business!" His students recalled the verse of Scripture: "I am eaten up with concern for my Father's fellowship."

18. So the church people challenged him, "Can you prove that you have the right to act in this way?" Jesus replied, "Pull down this sanctuary, and in three days I will raise it." The church members answered, "It took forty-six years to build this sanctuary, and you are going to raise it in three days?" The sanctuary he was talking about, however, was his body. And when he was raised from the dead, his students recalled that he had said this, and they put their faith in Jesus' message, both written and spoken.

23. While he was in Atlanta for the annual convention, many people, upon seeing the convincing things he did, surrendered themselves to him. On the other hand, Jesus never did surrender himself to them, simply because he knew everybody and because he didn't need information from anyone about a person, since he already knew the inside of a man.

3.

1. Now there was a very prominent churchman by the name of Nicodemus. This man came to Jesus one night and said, "Professor, we are aware that you are an inspired teacher, because nobody could present the marvelous things you're presenting without God's help."

"I want to make it clear," Jesus answered, "that *no one* can be a member of God's family unless he is fathered from above."

Nicodemus asked, "But how can a man be fathered once he is born? He can't return to his mother's womb and be re-fathered, can he?"

Jesus replied, "Except a person be fathered by both semen and Spirit, he can't be a member of God's family. Flesh fathers flesh, and Spirit fathers spirit. Don't be so surprised, then, that I told you that people have to be fathered from above. The wind[3] blows as it will, and you listen to its sound, but you have no idea where it's coming from or where it's going. It's like that when a person is fathered by the Spirit."[3]

9. "How can this possibly be true?" Nicodemus asked.

"Well, well," Jesus answered. "Here you are, 'the nation's foremost theologian,' and yet you don't grasp these things? I assure you that we speak and testify from firsthand knowledge and experience, but you folks won't accept our evidence. If I have used simple illustrations and you're not convinced, how would I ever persuade you with theological arguments?

13. "No one has penetrated the spiritual realm except the son of man, who came out of it. And just as Moses put a brass snake on a pole in the wilderness,[4] even so must the son of man be put on a pole, in order that all who trust him might have spiritual life. In the same way, God loved the world so much that he gave his only Son, that whoever trusts him might not die, but might have spiritual life. For God did not send his Son into the world to damn it, but that through him the world might be rescued. He who lives by him is not damned, but he who does not live by him is already damned, because he does not live up to the name of God's only Son. This is the damnation: The Light came into the world, and the people preferred the darkness to the Light, because their ways were wicked. For the person whose life is false shuns the Light and won't go near it, for fear that his ways will be rebuked. But the person whose life is true comes out into the Light, so that it might be clear that his ways are rooted in God."

22. Following this, Jesus and his students went to south Georgia, and he spent a while there with them and was doing some baptizing. John was baptizing at Eufaula near Georgetown, because there was plenty of water there, and people were coming to him and getting immersed. (This was before John had been thrown in jail.) Well, John's students and a Methodist got into a fuss over dipping and sprinkling. So they came to John and told him, "Reverend, you remember that fellow who was with you on the other side of the Chattahoochee, who you yourself praised? Guess what! Now he's dipping and everybody is joining up with *him!*" John answered, "A man can't take an office that hasn't been given him from above. You yourselves can bear me out that I told you, 'I am not the Leader, but I was sent ahead of him.' The man with the bride is the bridegroom. The best man stands with the groom and shares his joy. That's why I'm so happy. That man must grow, while I must fade out."

31. The one who springs from above is over everything. The earthling, being from the earth, speaks in terms of the earth. The spiritual person, however, is above all this. While he does talk about what he has seen and heard, nobody takes him seriously. When one does take him seriously, one becomes evidence that God is true. The God-sent man bears God's message, for God fully equips him with the Spirit. The Father loves the Son and has put him in charge of everything. When one lives by the Son, one has spiritual life. When one disobeys the Son, one won't catch a glimpse of life; rather, God's displeasure hangs over him.

4.

1. The word spread among the church people that Jesus was making and baptizing more converts than John. (Jesus himself, however, wasn't doing any baptizing, but his students were.) So when Jesus found out about this, he pulled out of south Georgia and headed again for north Georgia. On the way he had to go through a black ghetto. Well, he came to a black village named Sidecar, which is near the farm that Mr. Jake gave to his boy Joe. There's a well there called "Jake's well." So Jesus was pretty tired from traveling, and he sat like this on the curbing of the well. It was about noon. Now here comes a black woman to draw some water. Jesus says to her, "Please give me a drink." (His students had all gone to town to buy some food.)

Then she says to him, "How come a white man like you is asking for a drink from a black woman like me?" (Blacks and whites, you know, don't have much to do with one another.)

Jesus answers, "If you just knew God's goodness, and who it is asking you for a drink, *you* would ask *him* and he would give you *running* water."

She says, "Mister, that well is deep, and you don't even have a bucket. So where you gonna get running water? Do you have it over Grandpa Jake, who dug the well and used it for his family and livestock?"

Jesus replies, "When somebody drinks this water he gets thirsty again. When he drinks the water *I* give him, he'll never again get thirsty; in fact, the water I give someone becomes an inner-flowing spring, bubbling over with spiritual life."

The lady says to him, "Mister, gimme that water, so I won't get thirsty, and so I won't have to come back here to draw water!
"

He says to her, "Okay, go call your husband, and come here."

The lady answers, "I ain't got a husband."

Jesus says, "You're telling the truth when you say, 'I ain't got a husband,' because you've had *five* men, and the one you're living with now isn't your husband. You are absolutely correct."

The lady says, "Mister, I can tell that you're a preacher, right? Well, you know, my people have always said that the best time to worship God is Sunday afternoon, but you folks insist on Sunday morning at eleven."

"Listen here, ma'am," Jesus interrupts, "the time is coming when you'll worship the Father neither in the morning nor in the afternoon. You folks aren't sure about your worship; we white folks are, because we invented worship! Just the same, the time is coming—it's here already—when the sincere worshippers will worship the Father in spirit and with honesty. Indeed, the Father is looking for people like that to worship him. God is spirit, and when people worship him they must do it in spirit and with honesty."

The lady answers, "I realize that Christ (the word for Leader) is coming. When he does, he'll straighten us out on everything!"

Jesus says to her, "I myself, the person talking with you, am he!"

27. Along about this time, his students returned, and they were quite surprised that he was talking with a black woman, yet nobody asked, "What are you up to?" or "Why are you talking with her?" So the lady left her water bucket, checked out for town, and said to the men there, "Come and meet a fellow who told me everything I ever did. Do you suppose he might be the Leader?" They went tearing out of the city and came to him.

31. In the meanwhile, the students said to him, "Come on, Professor, let's eat."

He replied, "I have some food to eat that you don't know about."

Then the students started asking one another, "You reckon somebody brought him something to eat?"

Jesus told them, "My food is doing the Father's will and getting on with his work. You all say that the harvest is four months away, don't you? Well, listen to what I'm telling you: Open your eyes and look at those fields. Right now they are at the peak of harvesting. Already the Harvester is hired and he is gathering spiritual life fruit, so that the Planter and the Harvester may rejoice together. The statement about this is correct, because the Planter is one and the Harvester is another. And *I* sent *you* to harvest a crop that you haven't sweated over. Others put in the sweat, and you've reaped the benefit of it."

39. Many people of the black village trusted him simply on the grounds of the woman's statement that "he told me everything I ever did." So when the blacks gathered about him, they started asking him to spend a while with them. He did so, staying there two days. An even larger group put their faith in him on the basis of his own words. They told the woman, "Our faith is no longer based on your story alone, for we ourselves have heard him and are convinced that he is truly the world's deliverer."

43. At the end of the two days, he left there for north Georgia. (Jesus himself fully agreed that a true man of God has little or no influence among the folks back home.) So when he arrived in north Georgia, the people welcomed him. They had been at the Convention in Atlanta and had seen for themselves all that he had done. Well, he returned to Canton, where he had made the water into wine. There was this government bigwig who had a sick son in Savannah. Having heard that Jesus had arrived in north Georgia, he went to him and urged him to come over and heal his boy, who was in mighty bad shape. Jesus said to him, "Unless you all see signs and miracles, you just won't be trustful." The big man said, "Please, mister, come on before my boy dies!" Jesus told him, "Okay, you may go now; your boy is well." The fellow acted on Jesus' instructions, and went. As he was returning, some friends met him and said, "Your boy is well!" He then asked them what time his boy started to get better. "About one o'clock yesterday afternoon," they said, "the fever went away." The father recognized this as the exact time that Jesus had told him, "Your boy is well." So he surely put his faith in Jesus, and his whole family did, too. (This was the second sign that Jesus did after he moved from south Georgia to north Georgia.)

5.

1. After this, there was a church convention in Atlanta, and Jesus attended. Now, in Atlanta at Shepherd's Park there is a pool called Bethesda, which is surrounded by five pavilions. In these pavilions were many afflicted people—blind, crippled, paralyzed. One of them was a man who had been afflicted for thirty-eight years. When Jesus saw him lying there, and knowing that he had been in this condition for a long time, he said to him, "Would you like to get well?" The afflicted man answered, "Mister, I don't have a soul to help me get in the pool while the water is all stirred up. When I try to put myself in, somebody beats me there." Jesus said to him, "Get up, pick up your pallet, and start walking!" And right then the man was well, and he picked up his pallet and started walking!

10. But, it so happened that it was Sunday. So some good church people told the healed man, "Today is Sunday, and it isn't right for you to be moving furniture around." He replied, "Well, the same guy who made me well told me to pick up my pallet and start walking." They asked, "Who is the fellow who said for you to pick it up and start walking?" The healed guy really didn't know who it was because there was a big crowd and Jesus had gotten lost in it. But later on, Jesus found him in the church and said to him, "Look, you're well; don't let your life get messed up or something worse might happen to you." The man left, and told the church people that it was Jesus who had healed him. So they gave Jesus a fit for doing such things on a Sunday. Jesus' answer was, "My Father is working right on, so I'm working." For this they were trying all the more to kill him, not only because he broke the Sabbath, but because he called God his own father, thus making himself equal with God.

19. So Jesus really explained it to them. "Let me set you straight: The Son can't do anything on his own—only what he sees the Father doing. When he does something, the Son does the same thing. The Father likes the Son and shares with him his concerns, and, though it might surprise you, he will share his activity on an even larger scale. For example, even as the Father lifts up the dead and gives them newness of life, so will the Son, too, give newness of life to people of his choice. The Father isn't deciding on people; rather, he has referred every decision to the Son, so that all will respect the Son in the same way they respect the Father. When one disrespects the Son, one disrespects the Father who appointed him. Let me make it clear to you that the person who listens to my message and puts his faith in him who appointed me has spiritual life; this person is not called up for examination, but has transferred from the death region to the life region. I'm telling you, the time is coming—it's here already— when the lifeless ones will tune in to the voice of God's Son and, having heard him, will come alive. For as the Father is a life-bearer, so he has made the Son a life-bearer. He has also given him, as the son of man, the right to set up a standard. Don't let this surprise you, because the day is coming when the graveyard set will hear his voice and will move on out—those who have committed themselves to the right, into the celebration of life; those who have committed themselves to the wrong, into the celebration of damnation. I am unable to act on my own; I decide on the basis of what I hear, and my decisions are fair. I'm not out to have my own way, but to do what God wants.

31. "If I am my own witness, my testimony won't hold water. But someone else is my witness, and I'm convinced that his testimony about me will stand up. You all questioned John, and he gave you the honest truth. But even so, I'm not resting my case on human testimony; I'm just talking this way so that you might be straightened out. That guy, John, was turned on—a shining light—and you were willing to dance in his light for a little while. But I have even greater evidence than John's: the course of action that my Father gave me to carry out This program that I'm engaged in is evidence that the Father sent me So the same Father who sent me has himself testified in my behalf. The reason you've never heard his voice, or seen his face, or had his word to take root in you is that you're putting no trust in his appointed one. You do study the Bible, expecting to find spiritual life in it, and all the while it is loaded with evidence about me. *Yet*, you refuse to go my route to find life. I don't go in for human prestige, but I know full well that you've got no love of God in you. Here I come flying my Father's flag and you reject me. If somebody else came flying his own flag, you would accept him. How can you ever be people of faith when you accept credentials from one another, but don't even look at the credentials from the One God. Don't think that I'll be your accuser before God. Your accuser is that on which you pin your hopes—the Bible itself. For if you had *truly* believed the Bible, you would have had faith in me too, because it is written about me. But if you aren't living by what it tells *you*, how will you live by what I say?"

6.

1. Later on, Jesus crossed the big lake and was followed by a large crowd, because they saw the tremendous things he was doing for the sick. So Jesus climbed up the hill and sat down with his students around him. Now the annual Convention, the big meeting of the church people, was drawing near. Well, Jesus looked up and saw that a lot of people were coming to him, so he said to Phil, "How will we buy enough food to feed all these people?" (Since he already knew what he was about to do, he was sort of pulling Phil's leg.) Phil answered, "Even if everybody got only a taste, it would take about two hundred dollars' worth!" Then one of the students—Andy, Rock's brother—piped up, "There's a kid here who has five buns and two hot dogs, but that won't go a long way toward feeding this crowd!"

10. Jesus said, "Please tell the people to be seated." (There was a lot of grass at this spot.) So the crowd, numbering about five thousand, sat down, and Jesus took the buns, said grace, and served the seated people. He did the same with the hot dogs, and everybody took as many as they wanted. When they finished eating, Jesus told the students, "Y'all gather up the leftovers so we don't waste anything." They collected them, and even after the people had eaten all they could hold, there still were left twelve big basketsful of leftovers of the five buns.

Seeing him do such a tremendous thing, the people said, "There's no doubt about it, this is God's Man for the world!" And when Jesus realized that they were planning to draft him for governor, he checked out of there and again went into the mountain alone.

16. About sundown the students went down to the sea, got in a boat, and headed back toward Savannah. It had already gotten dark, and still Jesus hadn't joined them. A strong wind was blowing, causing the sea to swell. When they were three or four miles out, they saw Jesus walking on the sea and drawing near the boat, and it just about scared their pants off. "Hey, it's me!" he shouted. "Y'all stop being so scared." Well, they did agree to take him on board, and that quick the boat was at the land they were heading toward.

22. Next morning the crowd that had stayed on the other side of the sea noticed that only one little boat was left there. They knew that Jesus had not left in the boat with his students, but that they had gone away by themselves. However, some small boats from Tybee Island were near the spot where they had eaten the buns that Jesus had blessed. So when the crowd realized that neither Jesus nor his students were there, they clambered aboard the boats and went to Savannah looking for Jesus. Upon finding him over there they said, "Reverend, how did you get here?"

Jesus replied, "It's as clear as day that you are looking me up not because you're reading my signs but because you got your bellies full of buns. Don't busy yourselves with groceries but with the food that nourishes spiritual life, which the son of man will give you." (The Father-God authorized him to do this.)

So they asked him, "What shall we do to busy ourselves with God's business?"

Jesus answered, "God's business is this: that you live by him whom he sent."

Then they said, "Well, what evidence are you presenting that we can examine and that will cause us to trust you? What are you offering? Our ancestors, you know, were supplied with free food while they were in the desert, just as the Scripture says, 'He gave them bread from on high.'"

Jesus told them, "No, I'm telling you, Moses didn't give you the bread from on high; however, my Father does give you the real bread from on high; God's 'loaf' is the one who comes down from on high and gives the world life."

"Mister," they responded, "evermore load us up with this bread."

And Jesus said, "I, I am the 'loaf' of life. The man who takes my route will never go hungry, and the one who bases his life on mine will never stay thirsty.

36. "But as I told you, you have looked and still you aren't leaping. I'll take all that the Father gives me, and will by no means cast aside anyone who takes my route. I haven't come down from on high just to carry out my own desire but that of him who sent me. And what is his desire? That I should not let a single one of those he gave me slip through my fingers, but that I should give them newness of life in the final hour. It is also my Father's desire that everyone who really looks at the Son and takes the leap with him should have spiritual life, and I myself will make him new in the final hour."

41. Then the church people raised a stink because he said, "I myself am the 'loaf' that came down from on high." They said, "Why, isn't this old Joe's boy? Don't we ourselves know his mama and daddy? How come he now claims that 'I have come down from on high'?"

Jesus replied, "Y'all quit your bellyaching. Nobody can go with me unless the Father, who sent me, attracts him. And I'll make *him* new in the final hour. The Bible says, 'And all will be God-taught.' Anyone who listens and learns from the Father comes my way. It's not that a person has actually seen God. Only the One who is from the Father has done that. I truly tell you that he who lives his faith has spiritual life. I repeat, I myself am the 'loaf' of the life. Your ancestors did eat the free food in the desert—and they died! But *this* loaf has come down from on high so that a person might eat from it and *not* die. I am indeed the live loaf that came down from on high. If one eats from this loaf, he'll be alive in the new age. Now the loaf that I'll give for the life of the world is my own flesh."

52. Then the church people got into a big hassle with one another over this. "How can this cat give us his flesh to eat?" they asked.

So Jesus told them, "I want to make it clear to you that unless you eat the flesh and drink the blood of the son of man, you'll have no inner life. He who feasts on my flesh and drinks my blood has spiritual life, and I'll make him new in the final hour. My flesh is real food, and my blood is real drink. He who feasts on my flesh and drinks my blood lives on in me and I in him. Even as the living Father sent me, so does he sustain me. And the one who feasts on me will also be sustained by me. This, I say, is the 'loaf' that descended from on high. It is not like that which your ancestors ate and then passed on. He who feasts on *this* loaf will be alive in the new age." These words were spoken while he was teaching in the church at Savannah.

60. Well, upon hearing all this a good number of his students said, "This lesson is mighty hard to swallow. Who can take it?"

When Jesus realized that his students were griping about this, he said to them, "Does this gag you? What if you should see the son of man ascending to his former position? Listen, it is the *spirit* that makes a man alive; the *body* does nothing for him. It is *spirit* and *life* that I've been talking to you about, but some of you still don't go for it!" (Jesus knew all along who the ones were that would not go for it, and even who the person was that would turn him in.) He continued, "That's why I told you that nobody could come my way unless he were motivated by the Father."

66. At this point a lot of his students called it quits and dropped out. So Jesus said to the twelve, "Do you too want to leave?" "Sir," said Rock, "to whom shall we turn? You have the words of spiritual life. Besides, we have confidence and knowledge that *you* are God's special One " Jesus said to them, "Didn't I pick you twelve, and yet one of you is a devil?" (He was referring to Simon Iscariot's son, Judas, since he—one of the twelve—was on the verge of turning him in.)

7.

1. Following this, Jesus went on a tour of Alabama. He had no desire to tour Georgia, because the good white folks there were trying to kill him. There was a big revival going on in Atlanta, so Jesus' brothers said to him, "Say, why don't you pull out of here and go to Georgia so that all your cronies might keep up with your program. You know, nobody hides his light under a bushel if he wants to be well known. If you're so great, the whole world ought to know about it." (Even his own brothers had no faith in him.) So Jesus said to them, "My day isn't here yet, but your day is always handy. The world doesn't have the heart to hate you, but it does hate me because I show it up for what it is—and it stinks. So y'all run along to the revival. I'm not going to that revival, because my day just hasn't arrived." Having said this, he stayed on in Alabama.

10. But when his brothers actually did go to the revival, then Jesus went too, but secretly and not openly. The good white folks were trying to find him at the revival and were asking, "Where is that guy?" Quite an argument broke out among the crowd. Some said, "He's great." Others said, "Naw, he's an outside agitator." But nobody would express himself freely about him, because they were afraid of one another.

14. When the revival was about half over, Jesus went up to First Church and began teaching. The people were really amazed by him. "How can this guy be so educated without going to college?" they wondered.

Jesus replied, "I am not a self-educated man; my instruction came from him who sent me. If *anybody* truly wants to do God's will, he will be convinced as to whether this instruction is from God or whether I trumped it up myself. When a man spouts his own ideas, he is trying to get credit for himself. But when one seeks the credit of his sender, then he is honest and aboveboard. Look, you've been given the Bible, haven't you? But not a one of you lives by it! So why are you trying to kill me?"

The crowd answered, "You're crazy in the head; who's trying to kill you?"

"Just because I did some work on a Sunday you're all in a tizzy. All right, now listen. The Bible tells you to baptize—well, not exactly, but it is a Christian tradition—and you have no qualms about baptizing on a Sunday. If you break the Sabbath just to baptize a man, why are you bitching about my making a man well on the Sabbath? Don't hold to opinions because they're popular but because they're right."

25. Then some of the Atlantans said, "Isn't this the fellow they're trying to lynch? Well, what do you know, there he is preaching in public! Do you reckon the Establishment honestly believes that this cat is the Leader? Of course, where the Leader comes from nobody knows, but we do know where this man's from."

28. So while Jesus was teaching in the church he lowered the boom on them: "Okay, you know me and where I'm from. Yet you don't know the True One who sent me, or that I'm not on a mission of my own. I do know him, because I am from him and he sent me."

30. They set in to trap him, but nobody laid a finger on him because it wasn't yet his day. But on the other hand, a considerable number did come over to his side. "Suppose our great Leader should arise," they reasoned; "would he be able to do anything this man isn't doing?"

32. When the church people heard that his poll rating was rising, they got together with their officials and sent some hoods to rough him up. Then Jesus said, "I'll be with you a little while longer, and then I'm going to him who sent me. You'll look for me but won't find me, because I'll be where you can't come." The good white folks said to one another, "Where do you reckon he'll be going that *we* can't find him? Does he plan to go to the black ghettos and teach the blacks? What did he mean when he said, 'You'll look for me and won't find me, and I'll be where you can't come'?"

37. On the big day at the close of the revival, Jesus got up and shouted, "If anyone is thirsting, let him come to me and drink. From the heart of the man who lives, my life will flow, as the Bible says, floods of life-giving water." (He was referring to the Spirit, which those who live his life were to receive. There was not yet a Spirit because Jesus still hadn't brought things to a climax.)

40. The crowd's reaction to his message varied. Some said, "There's no doubt about it; this is the Man of God." Others agreed, "He is the heaven-sent Leader." But some weren't so sure. "The heaven-sent Leader isn't a hillbilly, is he? Doesn't the Bible

predict that he'll come from an old-line family in south Georgia?"
So the crowd was split over him. Some of them even wanted to
lynch him, but nobody put their cotton-pickin' hands on him.

45. Well, the hoods went back to the religious people who
had sent them, and were asked, "Why didn't you tend to him?"
The hoods replied, "There ain't *never* been a cat that talks like
that cat." The church people answered, "Have you too been
duped? Have any important people or church members come
over to him? But this ragtag and bobtail, who don't understand
the Bible, are going to hell." Nicodemus, who was one of them
and who had previously come to Jesus, asked them, "Does our
Bible condemn a man without letting him state his case or
inquiring into what he is doing?" They hushed him up, saying,
"So you're a hillbilly too, huh? Look it up for yourself and you'll
see that no hillbilly was ever a man of God." They stalked out and
went home.

8.

1. Then Jesus went out to Peach Orchard Hill.[5] Early next
morning he returned to First Church, where a crowd gathered
and he began teaching them. Then some preachers and members
of the official board led in a lady caught having sex with someone
she wasn't married to. They stood her up front and said to Jesus,
"Professor, this woman was caught in the act of extramarital sex.
Now our Bible specifically condemns such an act. What do you
say about it?" (They were trying to frame him so they would have
something to charge him with.) Jesus looked down and wrote in
the sand with his finger. And when they kept on pestering him,
he glanced up and said, "Okay, let the man whose heart is pure
lead off." He looked down again and kept writing in the sand.
They got the point and, beginning with the elders, they sneaked

out one by one, until only Jesus was left with the lady standing in front of him. He looked up and said to her, "Where did they all go, ma'am? Didn't *anybody* condemn you?" She said, "Not a soul, sir." Jesus said, "Well, I surely don't condemn you. Run along now, and don't do it again."

12. Once more Jesus was telling people, "I am the light of the world. He who lets me lead him will never stumble in the dark, but will have life's light."

The church people said to him, "Now you're blowing your own horn. What you're saying just isn't so."

"All right," Jesus answered, "even if I am blowing my own horn, I'm telling the truth, because I know where I came from and where I'm going. But you all know neither of these things about me. You measure by human standards; I don't measure anybody. But even if I should measure a man, I would do so honestly, because I wouldn't do it alone but with him who sent me. Even in your Bible it says that the evidence of two witnesses is reliable. Now, I'm testifying in my own behalf, and the Father who sent me is also testifying for me."

"Where is your father?" they asked.

"You don't understand me," he answered, "and you don't understand my Father. If you had understood me, you would have understood my Father." This discussion took place while Jesus was teaching in the church basement. And nobody arrested him because it just wasn't his day yet.

21. Again Jesus told them, "I'm leaving and you'll look for me, and you'll rot in your mess. You can't come where I'm going."

The good white folks said, "Do you reckon he's considering suicide—talking about 'you can't come where I'm going'?"

He replied, "Y'all take the human point of view; I, the divine. You belong to the old order; I don't. That's why I told you that you would rot in your mess. And rot in your mess you will unless you wake up to who I am."

"Who are you?" they asked.

"I am what I've been telling you all along. I have many things about you to tell and discuss. He who sent me is for real, and I am repeating in the world what I've heard from him." (They still didn't understand that he was talking to them about the Father.) "When you respect the son of man, then you will know who I am and that I do nothing on my own. I speak only the things my Father taught me. And he who sent me backs me up and doesn't leave me alone, because I am always engaged in the things he wants."

30. These words convinced many to come over to him. So Jesus said to the good white folks who had come over to him, "If y'all stick by what I've said, you are honest followers of mine. You'll understand the truth, and the truth will liberate you."

They responded, "But we are blue-blooded white folks, and have never been *anybody's* slave. Why, then, are you telling *us*, 'You'll be liberated'?"

Jesus answered, "Everyone who is addicted to sin is sin's slave. Now the slave never lives in 'the big house'; the free-born son lives there. So then, if the Son liberates you, you're genuinely liberated. I know that you are blue-blooded white folks, but just the same you're trying to do me in because my ideas don't appeal to you. I'm preaching what I've actually *seen* from the Father; but you, you're practicing what you've heard from your father."

"Our father was the original white man," they retorted.

"If indeed you are sons of the original white man, you would act like it. But here you are trying to lynch me, a man who has told you the truth that I got from the Father. A really good white man would *never* stoop to that. Yes, you're behaving like *your* father's children all right."

"We aren't bastards," they said. "The One God is our Father."

"If God were truly your Father," Jesus said, "you would love me, for God sent me and that's why I'm here. I haven't come simply of my own accord; God sent me. What's the matter? Aren't you catching on to what I'm saying? Perhaps it's because you can't take my ideas. You fellows are the sons of your daddy, the Confuser, and you are determined to carry out your daddy's desires. Well, your daddy has always been a man-killer, and has never sided with the truth, because there's no truth in him. When he tells a lie, he is simply repeating himself, because he's a liar and the daddy of liars. But when *I* tell you the truth you don't believe me. Can any of you prove me guilty of any wrongdoing? Okay, if I'm shooting straight, why don't you believe me? When a man is rooted in God, he pays attention to what God says. Since you don't pay attention, it is clear that you're not rooted in God."

48. The good white folks said, "We sure hit the nail on the head when we said that you are a nigger and are full of the Confuser." Jesus replied, "I am not full of the Confuser, but I do respect my Father, even though you all disrespect me. I'm not concerned about making a name for myself; however, there is One who is concerned about his name and has the final say-so. I tell you for a fact that if a person latches onto my idea, he will surely be immortal."

52. The good white folks shouted at him, "Now we're positively sure that you're full of the Confuser. Look, both the founder of our church and the old-time men of God passed away, yet you are saying, 'If a person latches onto my idea, he will surely be immortal.' Do you think you're greater than the noble founder of our church? Well, he died, as did the other church fathers. So what do you make of yourself?"

54. Jesus answered, "If I okay myself, my okay is no good. The one who okays me is my Father, who you claim is your God. But you have no knowledge of him. I do, though, and even if I said I didn't, I'd only be a liar like you. I truly do know him and I carry out his idea. Abraham, the founder of your church, was tickled pink that he should catch a glimpse of my rule—and he did see it and was delighted."

The good white folks said to him, "So you've seen Abraham even though you're not yet fifty?"

To this Jesus replied, "I existed before Abraham was born."

They picked up rocks to throw at Jesus, but he hid and then ducked out of the church.

Notes on John

[1] Or, son of John, or John's son; hence, Johnson.

[2] The Greek word here means to draw water from a well with a bucket. The sane word is used in John 4:7: "A woman from Samaria came to draw (or bucket up) water." Obviously, then, the servants got the water for the emcee from the same source as they got water to fill the jars—from the well. The *well* turned to wine, not the water in the stone jars. The same well which supplied water to fill full, or fulfill, the jars (the Mosaic laws), now supplies the good wine which delights the emcee. This first "sign" perhaps points to the fact that the same God (the well) who gave the law on Sinai, now fulfills it by giving grace (the wine as a symbol of shed blood) on Calvary. Men taste of and say, "It's good," but they taste of grace and say, "You've saved the best till last."

[3] There is a play on words here, since the same Creek word can mean either *wind* or *spirit*.

[4] See Numbers 21:4-9.

[5] Verses 1-11 of this chapter are not supported by the most reliable manuscripts as part of the original text. The story is so moving, however, that I am including it anyway.